I0138300

Regeneration and the New Birth

By Isaac Ambrose

Regeneration and the New Birth
By Isaac Ambrose

Edited and updated by C. Matthew McMahon and Therese B. McMahon
Transcribed by Scott Truax

Some language and grammar has been updated from the original manuscript. Any change in wording or punctuation has not changed the intent or meaning of the original author(s), and has been made to aid the modern reader.

Published by Puritan Publications
A Ministry of A Puritan's Mind
4101 Coral Tree Circle #214
Coconut Creek, FL 33073
www.puritanshop.com
www.apuritansmind.com
www.puritanpublications.com

This Print Edition, 2012
Electronic Edition, 2012
Manufactured in the United States of America

ISBN: 978-1-938721-93-9
eISBN: 978-1-938721-92-2

TABLE OF CONTENTS

MEET ISAAC AMBROSE

Isaac Ambrose (1604–1663), was a Lancashire divine whose works were long held in esteem. He was descended from the Ambroses of Lowick, Furness, and was baptized May 29, 1604 at Ormskirk, where his father was vicar. He entered Brasenose College, Oxford, 1621, in 1624 he proceeded to earn a B.A., and having been ordained was presented by Bishop Morton to the "little cure" of Castleton, Derbyshire, 1627. Ambrose attracted the notice of William Russell, afterwards earl of Bedford, and was by the king's influence incorporated at Cambridge University from 1631 to 1632. Having resigned his small living in 1631, he was made one of the king's four preachers in Lancashire, and took up his residence at Garstang. About the year 1640 the interest of the religious Lady Margaret Hoghton obtained for him the vicarage of the corporate town of Preston in Amounderness. In November of 1642 he was for a time taken prisoner by the king's commissioners of array, and he was again arrested March 20, 1643; but in both cases was released by the influence of neighboring gentlemen. On the arrest of Robert Bolton in May 1644, he took refuge at Leeds. He associated himself with the establishment of Presbyterianism in the county, and held important positions by the favor of the House of Commons and his neighboring brethren. Having set his hand to the "Agreement of the People taken into consideration," the committee of plundered ministers ordered him to be sent a prisoner to London (April and May 1649), where he made the acquaintance of Lady Mary Vere and other persons, who, with the Earl of Bedford, relieved his necessities. He was still the "painful" minister of Preston in 1650. The prominent connection of this town with the war, and the strong party feelings of the inhabitants, led him to remove to Garstang in 1654; and then, in 1662, he was ejected for nonconformity. Ambrose was himself a Puritan and a Presbyterian, seen clearly when he subscribed to the *Solemn League and Covenant* of 1643, and he was one of the ministers who served on the committee of Parliament appointed to oversee the ejection of "scandalous and ignorant ministers and schoolmasters" during the Commonwealth. Having retired to Preston, he died suddenly of apoplexy in 1663, and was buried January 25th.

The works of Isaac Ambrose:

He wrote "Prima, Media, and Ultima," 4to, 1650, 1659; a funeral sermon on "Redeeming the Time" (on Lady Hoghton), 1658, 4to; "Looking unto Jesus," 1658, 4to; "War with Devils — Ministration of Angels," 1661, 4to. These were reprinted in folio, with a portrait, 1674, 1682, 1689; and the smaller treatises have frequently been reprinted. He has letters prefixed to some of the works of his friend Henry Newcome. "Ambrose," says Emund Calamy, "was a man of that substantial worth, that eminent piety, and that exemplary life, both as a minister and a Christian, that it is to be lamented the world should not have the benefit of particular memoirs of him." His character has been misrepresented by Mr. Wood. He was of a peaceful disposition; and though he put his name to the fierce "Harmonious Consent," he was not naturally a partisan. He evaded the political controversies of the time. His gentleness of character and earnest presentation of the gospel attached him to his people. He was much given to secluding himself, retiring every May into the woods of Hoghton Tower and remaining there a month. Dr. Halley justly characterizes him as the most meditative puritan of Lancashire. This quality pervades his writings, which abound, besides, in deep feeling and earnest piety. Mr. Hunter has called attention to his recommendation of diaries as a means of advancing personal piety, and has remarked, in reference to the fragments from Ambrose's diary quoted in the "Media," that "with such passages before us we cannot but lament that the carelessness of later times should have suffered such a curious and valuable document to perish."

For further study:

Wood's *Ath. Oxon.* (ed. Bliss), iii. 659, and *Fasti.* i. 414; Calamy's *Abridgement of Baxter* (1713), 409, and Contin. 566; Newcome's *Autobiog.* and *Diary passim*; *Faringdon Papers*, 107; Halley's *Lanc. Nonconformity*, i. 194 seq.; Chetham's *Ch. Libraries*, p. 170; Fishwick's *Hist. of Garstang*, 161 seq.; Cox's *Derbyshire Churches*, iv. 499.

PART 1:
THE DOCTRINE OF REGENERATION

"Except a Man be born again, he cannot see the Kingdom of God." John 3:3.

In the prosecution of these words, we shall follow the order set down by the Holy Spirit where we *find:*

1. Its Necessity.
2. Its Generality.
3. Its Manner.
4. Its Issue.

First, its necessity: *Except a man be new born*, he can never be saved. It is our Savior's speech, and he presses it emphatically, *Verily, verity, I say unto thee.*

Again, God the Father in this way counsels, not only Nicodemus, but all the Jews of the old church, saying, "Make yourself a new heart and a new spirit, for why will you die, O house of Israel?" (Ezek. 18:31). Notwithstanding all their privileges, yet here is one thing necessary that must crown all the rest: they must have a *new* heart, and a *new* spirit, that is, they must be born again, or there is no way but death.

Nor, is this doctrine without reason or ground. For, man is first unholy, and therefore most unfit to enter into heaven. Without holiness no man shall see God, (Heb. 12:14). And what is man before he is new born? If we look on his soul, we may see it deformed with sin, defiled with lust, outraged with passions; and so is the image of God transformed to the ugly shape of the devil. Should we take a more particular view, every faculty of the soul is full of iniquity. The understanding understands nothing of the things of God; (*cf.* 1 Cor. 2:14). The will wills nothing that is good, (Rom. 6:20). The affections affect nothing of the Spirit (Gal. 5:17). In a word, the understanding is darkened, the will enthralled, the affections disordered, the memory defiled, the conscience benumbed, all the inner man is full of sin, and here is no part that is good, no not one. How needful now is a new birth to a man in this case? Can he enter into heaven that savors all of the earth? Will those precious gates of gold and pearls open to a *sinner*? No, he must be newly molded, and sanctified.

Secondly, without this, man is God's enemy; no greater opposition than between God and a sinner can exist; God's name and nature is altogether opposite to sin and sinners. We view those attributes of God, his justice, truth, patience, holiness, anger, power, *etc.*; his justice in punishing the impenitent according to his deserts, his truth effecting those plagues which he has spoken in his time, his patience forbearing sin's destruction, until they are grown fully ripe, his holiness abhorring all impurities, his anger stirring up revenge against all offered injuries, his power mustering up his forces, yes, all his creatures against his enemies. And what can we say if all these attributes are at enmity with sinful man, *woe to man because of offences.* Better he had never been born, than not to be born anew.

Thirdly, except by a new birth, man is *without* Christ. If any man is in Christ, he is a new creature. And if he is not in Christ, what hopes is there for that man? It is only Christ that opens heaven, it is only Christ that is the way to heaven, besides him there is no way, no truth, no life.

Fourthly, except a man is born again, he is a limb of Satan, a child of darkness, and one of the family of hell. Consider this, you that are out of the state of grace, in what miserable thralldom are your souls? Should any call you servants, you would take it highly in disdain. But take it as you please, if you are not regenerate, you are in no better case. Paul appeals to your own knowledge. "Know ye not, that to whom ye yield yourselves servants to obey, his servants ye are to whom ye obey; whether of sin unto death, or of obedience unto righteousness?" (Rom. 6:16). Then, "...the wages of sin is death; but the gift of God is eternal life through Jesus Christ our Lord," (Rom. 6:23). If then you obey the devil's suggestions, what are you but the devil's servants? And if he is your master, what are your wages? "The wages of sin is death," death of the body, and death of the soul. Death here, and death hereafter in hell-fire. Alas, that Satan should have this power on man! That he who is the enemy, and means nothing to a sinner but death and damnation, should be his *lord*, and tyrannize over him at his own will and pleasure! Would any man be lured to serve lions and tigers? And is not the devil a roaring lion, walking bout, and seeking whom he may devour? To serve him that would devour his servant, is a most miserable bondage; and what pay can one expect from devils, but roaring and devouring, and tearing souls?

Whether we consider man in regard of himself, or of God, or of Christ, or of Satan, he is, *except he is born again*, unholy, God's *enemy*, *out* of Christ, and *in Satan*.

And if the new birth is so necessary, how should we labor to be born again? Now then, as you tender your souls, and desire heaven as your ends, endeavor to attain this one thing necessary: lift up your hearts to God, that you may be washed, justified, sanctified in the name or the Lord Jesus. And that by "the Spirit" of God you may walk in new ways, talk with new tongues, as being new creatures, created to good works. So you would wait on God in his way, I trust the Lord in mercy would remember you, and his Spirit would blow on you, and then you would find and feel such a change within you, as that you would bless God forever, that you were in this way born again.

Man Must be Born Again

Such is the necessity of being born again. And as to the generality of it, all men, or all mankind must be regenerated before they are saved; not one of all the sons of Adam shall ever go to heaven, except he is born again. Let your contemplations guided by God's word, go into the paradise above; all the saints that now walk in its light, were first purged by the lamb, and sanctified by the Spirit; first they were regenerated, and so they were saved.

Universal Change in His Nature

Secondly, as all men, so all men, all the members of his body, all the faculties of his soul, must be changed. Sanctification, if saving, must be perfect and entire, though not in respect of degrees, yet in respect of parts; every part and power of body and soul must have its parts of sanctification.

And should we consider man in his parts, every part must bear a part in this birth. His body must be regenerated, and his soul must be renewed. He is molded anew, and all the members of his body are conformed to the sovereignty and rule of grace; yes, his body is preserved blameless, holy, and acceptable to God. It is a member of Christ, the temple of the Holy Spirit. Happy is the man that is blessed with this body in this way! Surely, a man in this way born again shall see the kingdom of God.

Secondly, as the body, so the soul of this man is to be renewed by grace. Therefore glorify God in your body and your spirit, (*cf.* 1 Cor. 6:20). The body and the spirit must both glorify God; and as all the parts of the body, so all the powers of the soul must do the same.

First, the *understanding*, that in the old man is blind and ignorant about heavenly things, or if it knows many things, yet can never attain to a saving knowledge. The new man must be anointed with the eye-salve of the Spirit, inspired with the knowledge of divine truths, especially with those sacred and saving mysteries which concern the kingdom of God. Again, the will that in the old man affects nothing but vile and vain things, is froward and perverse in the ways of godliness. The new man must prove what is the good, acceptable and perfect will of God; yes, it must attend and be subordinate to the grace of God, since God indeed, and God only, works in us both the will and the deed, (Phil. 2:13). Again, the memory that is in the old man is slippery in the things of God, or if naturally good, yet not spiritually useful. The new man must be sanctified to good performances; and although it cannot increase to a great natural perfection (for grace does not do this), yet the perfection it has must be straight, and right, and guided *Godward.* "Remember the Lord your God," Moses says, (Deut. 8:18). Again, the conscience that in the old man sleeps and slumbers, or if it is awake, tears and roars, as if a legion of devils possessed it. The new man must be calm and quiet; and yet not sleep or slumber, but rather in a friendly loving manner check and control wherever sin is, yes never be quiet, until with kind and yet earnest expostulations, it draws the sinner before God to confess his fault, and to seek pardon for it. Again, the affections that are in the old man are sensual, inordinate, bewitched; and set on wrong objects. The new man must be turned another way. To sum up everything, all must be renewed, the understanding, will, memory, conscience, and affections.

The Understanding must be Renewed

First, I say, in the new man the understanding must be renewed; so the apostle says, "The new man is renewed in knowledge," Col. 3:10; and this knowledge implies two habits, wisdom and prudence, (Col. 1:9). First wisdom, that is speculative, secondly, prudence, and that is practical. By the one, the child of God having the eyes of his mind opened and enlightened, sees the mysteries of salvation, the secrets of the kingdom, the whole counsel and the wonders of the Law of God. By the other he is enabled, with a judicious sincerity, to determine in the case of conscience and in the practice of piety, and the experimental passages of a Christian man. If we consider the first (*wisdom*), how is it possible that an unregenerate man should know the mysteries of salvation? He may go as far as the power of natural discourse, and light of reason can bear sway, he may be furnished with a store of rare and excellent learning, and yet for all this, lack true spiritual wisdom. The regenerate man has the saving knowledge, and he only knows God with a steadfast apprehension. He only knows himself as a mean, base, and contemptible thing. His new birth has taught him how wicked a creature he naturally is, and therefore in that respect he is odious to himself, and loathsome in his own eyes. Or if we consider the second, (*prudence*), how is it possible that an unregenerate man should experimentally know the practice of piety? Should we give an example in this mystery of regeneration: here is a ruler of the Jews (*Nicodemas*), and a teacher of Israel; yet as learned as he was, if he confers with Christ about the salvation of his soul, he is strangely childish, and a mere infant. Tell him of the new birth, and he thinks it is impossible, as for an old man to return into his mother's womb, and be born. The natural man cannot discern the operations of grace. He does not know that dark and fearful passage which leads from the state of nature, into the rich and glorious happiness of the kingdom of Christ. And here it is that many silly men or women, whom the worldly wise pass by with scorn, are more wise and learned in spiritual affairs than the most learned doctors of doctrines.

The Will Must Be Renewed

Secondly, the will must be renewed; and this will of the regenerate contains two things, righteousness and readiness. It is first rectified, conformed to the will of God. Secondly, it is so inflamed with the love of goodness, that he pursues it with alacrity of spirit. If we consider the first (the rectitude of the *will*), we see by experience the will of the unregenerate is all out of course. He wills nothing but that which is evil. How should he, considering his lack of God's perfect image, his blindness of heart, his proneness to evil, together with the vehemence of his affections, which draw the will after them? But in the man that is regenerate, the will being moved, it afterwards moves itself, God's grace that concurs with it quickens it, and revives it. So that now his will is nothing but God's will. Or if we consider the second, (the readiness of the will to good), alas! the will of the unregenerate has no pleasure in goodness, he does not understand the sweetness of it, and therefore nothing is more irksome to him than the ways of godliness. Whereas the will of the regenerate is willing, and this willingness indeed is the perfection of his will.

The Memory Must Be Renewed

Thirdly, the memory must be renewed; and this memory reflects occasionally on a double object, on God, and the things of God. First, on God, by remembrance of his presence everywhere. Secondly, on the things of God, by calling them to mind at useful times. If we consider the *first object*, God, the unregenerate has no mind on God. God is not in any of his thoughts, like the hood-winked fool that seeing nobody with his eyes closed, thinks nobody sees him. So he has said in his heart, *How does God know? Can he judge through the dark cloud?* Thick clouds are a covering to him that he does not see, and he walks in the circuit of heaven. But contrary to this, the regenerate man remembers his Creator in the days of his youth. And though God, as being a spirit, is absent from his senses, yet by virtue of his sanctified memory (that makes things absent as present), his eye is on God, and he considers

God as an eye-witness of all his thoughts and words and doings. Or, if we consider the second object (the word of God), the unregenerate never burdens his memory with it; if sometimes he comes across it, it is either by constraint, or by accident, never with any settled resolution to follow it. But the soul that is regenerate, with Mary, keeps all these things in his heart. Whatever lessons he learns, like so many jewels in a casket, he lays them up safe, and as need serves, makes all the good use of them that he may.

The Conscience Must Be Renewed

Fourthly, the conscience must be renewed, and that two ways, either by drawing the soul to good, or from evil. First, to good, by restraining and bridling. If we consider its first office (in that it draws and leads the soul to good), the unregenerate does not have that conscience; for the most part his conscience lies dead in his bosom, or if it stirs sometimes, he labors all he can to smother it. It is otherwise with the regenerate, his conscience excites him to do good, and he does good out of conscience. He does not stand on terms of pleasure or profit, but his conscience is being guided by the rule of God's holy truth, and he submits to it merely out of his obedience to God. It is here that *comes what will come*, his eye is fixed on God. And if man opposes where God commands, he is quickly resolved. Or if we consider the second office of conscience (in drawing the soul from evil), the unregenerate either does not hear, or does not heed his reclaiming conscience. If it speaks, he first goes about to lull it asleep again. Or if it cries out, and will not give him peace, then, (in spite of goodness), he runs out of one sin into another, and usually from presumption to despair. On the other side, the regenerate has a conscience that draws him from, and keeps him out of evil. It is known especially by these two properties, remorse and tenderness. Remorse has an eye on all sins past, and tenderness has an eye on all sins to come. By remorse is bred sorrow for sin, and loathing of sin. No sooner, he considers how by his manifold sins he has offended God, crucified Christ, grieved the Holy Spirit, but his heart bleeds and breaks that he has done so wickedly against so gracious a God. This sorrow for sin brings with it a loathing of sin. He hates the very thought of it. Every look-back is a new addition of detestation, and every meditation makes the wound of his remorse to bleed again. By tenderness of conscience is bred a care and watchfulness to avoid sin to come; for no sooner is sin presented to his conscience, but he startles at its sight, and meditates on that strict account he must one day make for it. Which, when thoughts and sin are put together in the balance, he does not dare do wickedly for a world of gain. And you may observe it, this tenderness (or easiness to bleed at the apprehension of sin), is peculiar to that conscience that is enlightened, and sanctified, and purged by Christ.

The Affections Must Be Renewed

Fifthly, the affections must be renewed, and that is done by setting them on right objects. I shall give you examples for some of them, as love, hatred, hope, fear, joy, sorrow, *etc.* I place love first, which in the unregenerate man is fastened inordinately on the creature; and as one sin begets another, so on whatsoever object it falls, it obtains some sin. So, the love of riches breeds covetousness, love of beauty breeds sensuality. Whatsoever he loves (the object being earthly), it brings with it some sin, and by it (the worst of all), he wickedly prefers earth to heaven, a dunghill to paradise. But the regenerate man settles his love on other objects; as he that is carnal, minds things carnal, so he that is spiritual, loves things spiritual. No sooner is he turned (by a sound and universal change of the whole man), from darkness to light, and from the power of Satan to God, but he presently begins to settle with some sweet contentment on the flowers of paradise, saving graces, and his infinite love runs higher and higher until it embraces him that dwells in the highest, God Almighty. And how sweet is that love that casts itself wholly into the heart of his Maker? How blessed is that man, that yearns, and melts, and cleaves, and clings to his gracious God above everything.

The second affection is hatred, which in the unregenerate is so inordinate, that he is a hater of God, (*cf.* Rom. 1:30). Not that he hates God in himself, but in some particular respect, because he restrains him from his pleasure, or punishes him for his sin, or crosses his appetites by his holy commands. And as he hates God, so likewise his brother. Here arise those envies, emulations, jars, contentions among those that profess themselves Christians. But of all brethren he hates them most, of whom our Savior is the first-born. God's faithful ones ever were and ever will be signs and wonders, and monsters to many, a scorn, reproach, and derision to them that are round about them. But he that is regenerate hates sin in whomsoever it rules, in others, and in himself, when after the commission of any evil he begins to repent, and to abhor himself (as Job did), in "dust and ashes," (Job 42: 6).

The third affection is hope. Now this hope in the unregenerate is fastened on this world, and the things of this world. He hopes for preferment, riches, or the like; as for his hopes of heaven, it is but a waking man's dream; *a dream*, I said? Yes, as dreams in the night fill us with illusions. You know a beggar may dream he is a king, so hope. Abusing the imagination of the unregenerate fills their souls many times with vain, or empty contentments; but the hope of the regenerate both enjoys the right object, and right means. His eye is fixed on future good; and he-endeavors to pursue it until he gets the possession. If in the pursuit he meets with crosses, griefs, disgraces, sicknesses, or any other calamities, his hope is able to sweeten the bitterest misery that can possibly befall him; the afflictions of this life bid him to look for a better life; a cross here minds him of the glory above.

The fourth affection is fear, which in the unregenerate is either worldly or servile if it fastens on the world, then he fears the loss of his credit or of his profit, and because he and the world must part at last, he fears this separation above all fears. O death, (the wise man says), how bitter is the remembrance of you to a man that lives at rest in his possessions, to the man that has nothing to vex him, and that has prosperity in all things? Or if his fear reflects on God, then it is a servile fear; for as the servant of a hireling does not work for love of his master, but only for fear of punishment, so he fears God for fear of punishment due to him from God. It is otherwise with the man that is born again; his fear is either initial or filial. It is either in pangs of the new birth, or in the new-born babe, it is called initial because then he casts away sin both out of God's love, to which he has partly attained, and out of the woeful effects of sin which he has thoroughly considered. With the right eye he beholds God, and with the left eye he beholds punishment so that this fear is a middle (as it were), between servile and filial fear. And as the needle draws in the thread, so this fear draws in charity and makes way for filial fear, to which, if by growth in grace he is fully ripened. Then he fears God out of love to God, as the prophet Isaiah proclaims, "And wisdom and knowledge shall be the stability of thy times, and strength of salvation: the fear of the LORD is his treasure," (Isa. 33:6). Never was a treasure more dear to the worldlings than is God's fear to him. His love of God, his desire to please God, and his fear of being separated from God, keep him in such awe, that though no punishment, no death, no hell were there at all, yet he would not sin for a world of treasures.

The fifth affection is worldly joy which in the unregenerate is sensual and brutish. It has no better objects than, gold, greatness, honors, or the like. And what are all these but a shadow, a ship, a bird, an arrow, a post that passes by. Or rather, as a crackling of thorns under a pot, as flashes of lightning before everlasting fire? But the joy of the regenerate is a spiritual joy, and the matter of it is the light of God's countenance, righteousness, or the promises of God's word. Or he sees above all, God Almighty blessed forever more. So David says, "Whom have I in heaven but thee? and there is none upon earth that I desire beside thee," (Psa. 73:25). This is that joy which no man can conceive, but he that enjoys it. This is that white stone, (Rev. 2:17), whose splendor shines only on heavenly hearts. This is that glimpse of heaven's glory, which springing up in a sanctified heart, out of the wells of salvation, and carried along with addition of fresh comforts (from the word and sacraments), through a fruitful current and the course of men's life, at last falls into the boundless and bottomless ocean of the joys of heaven.

The sixth affection is sorrow, which in the unregenerate is a worldly sorrow, and the effects of it are death; so the apostle says, "the sorrow of the world worketh death," (2 Cor. 7:10). In this kind, how endless are the sorrows of men for their losses or crosses, that may befall them. And howsoever some may endeavor to comfort them in Christ, nothing can relish with them that concerns heaven or salvation. But in the regenerate, the beholding of sin breeds sorrow, and the Apostle calls this *godly sorrow*, working repentance to salvation, not to be repented of.

Examine then yourselves, you that desire heaven as your ends. Would you inherit the kingdom? Would you live with angels? Would you save your souls? Examine and try whether your bodies and souls are sanctified; and if you have no sense or feeling of the new birth, (for it is a mystery to the unregenerate), they never look to see in (that state), the kingdom of God. But if you perceive the working of saving grace effectually in you, (and you cannot but perceive it if you have it), if you feel the power of godliness first seizing the heart, and after dispersing itself over all the parts and powers of body and soul, if your hearts are softened by the Spirit, if your eyes wait on God, if your ears listen to his Word, if your tongues show forth his praise, if your understandings attain to saving knowledge, if your wills conform to the will of God, if your memories are stored with heavenly doctrine, if your consciences are tender and sensible of the least sin, if you love that which is good, if you hate that which is evil, if you hope for the blessings above, if you fear him that can destroy both body and soul...in a word, *if you joy in goodness, if you sorrow for sin, then you are born again.* Happy is the man in this case that was ever born; and so every man must be, if he cannot be happy. Except a man, (every man, every part of man), be born again, he cannot see the kingdom of God.

The Manner

We come now to speak of the manner of it.

Except a man *be* regenerated, or begotten (saith Valla), as man that is born of a woman, is begotten of a man, so he that is born again, *must have a begetting too.* If you ask of whom is the new man begotten? James tells you, "Of his own will begat he us with the word of truth, that we should be a kind of firstfruits of his creatures," (James 1:18). The former words denote the impulsive cause, the latter the instrument; it was God that begat us, and with the seed of the word.

It was the Father, Son, and Holy Spirit, but in respect of the last act, it is of the Holy Spirit, and not of the Father, or the Son; and so our Savior concludes, John 3:6, 8, "That which is born of the Spirit, is spirit...and so is every man that is born of the Spirit."

Secondly, as God's Spirit is the principal, so God's word is the instrumental cause of our regeneration. "Being born again, not of corruptible seed, but of incorruptible, by the word of God, which liveth and abideth for ever," (1 Pet. 1:23). The author of the Hebrews says, "For the word of God is quick, and powerful, and sharper than any two-edged sword, piercing even to the dividing asunder of soul and spirit, and of the joints and marrow, and is a discerner of the thoughts and intents of the heart," (Heb. 4:12). They that are born again, cannot but remember how quick and powerful, and sharp God's word was at their regeneration. First, like a hammer it beat on their hearts until it broke them all to pieces, and than like a sword, by a terrible cutting, piercing power, it struck a shaking and trembling into the very center of their souls. Last of all, like oil it began to supple their wounds, and to heal their bruises, and to refresh the weak and tender heart with all the promises of God revealed in Christ.

And so a man being begotten of the spirit with the word of truth, he comes at last to the birth; to be born again, to be born after the spirit; and this is that second birth. A man is first born of the flesh, and he must be again born of the Spirit.

Here appears the difference of the first and second birth, the first birth is of the earth, and the second birth is of the Lord, from heaven. The first birth is of nature, full of sin as a result of the fall of Adam and the break in the covenant. The second is of grace, full of sanctity, filled with Christ, the second Adam, and the Covenant of Grace. The first birth is originally of flesh and blood, the second birth is originally of the Spirit and water. In a word, the first birth kills, the second gives life. Generation lost us, it must be *regeneration* that recovers us. O blessed birth, without which no birth is happy, in comparison of which (though it were to be born the heir of the whole world), all is but misery!

As to the new birth itself, I know it is not worked in all after one manner, nor is the manner known to us, but only so far as it is sensible in us, and therefore we must consider man before baptism, in baptism, and after baptism.

In some the new birth is worked before baptism as in the eunuch under Candace, Queen of the Ethiopians, (Acts 8:37). and in Cornelius, together with his kinsmen and near friends, (Acts 10:47), and so our charity wants to tell us that every covenant infant dying before baptism is renewed by the Spirit. But we must yield to the manner of God's working, we do not know, for it is the secret of the Spirit of God.

In others the new birth is worked at the moment of baptism, which indeed is the sacrament of the new birth and seal of regeneration. But howsoever we see the outward seal, yet we do not see the manner of the inward working. For this also is the secret of the Spirit of God.

In others the new birth is wrought after baptism; for whenever men receive Christ by faith, then do they feel the power of God regenerate them, and work all things in them which he offered in baptism. Now the manner of this reeling in, or of God's Spirit working, proceeds usually in this way. There are certain steps by which it passes; and howsoever in those whom God has blessed with great favor of holy education, the Spirit of God dropping grace into their hearts by various times, these steps or degrees are not so easily perceived. Yet in those men who have lived long in sin, no sooner do they come to a new birth but they can feel grace work in them step after step. And these steps we shall break down to the number of eight.

Step One

The first is *a sight of sin*, and this our Savior reckons the first work of the Spirit. "And when he is come, he will reprove the world of sin, and of righteousness, and of judgment," (John 16:8). He does this *of sin*, but how? Why, in this way: no sooner begins this blessed change from nature to grace but the conscience, worked on by God's word, opens its book, and presents the soul a roll of those many mighty, heinous *sins*, committed against God and man. There he may read in bloody burning lines the abominations of his youth, the sins of all his life. He then brings them into method, and the commandments of God stand as a remembrance before his eyes. The first tells him of his loving something above God. The second, of his worshipping a false god, or a true God after a false manner. The third, of his dishonoring the great and mighty name of God. The fourth, of his breaking the Lord's day, either in doing the works of the flesh, or leaving undone the works of the Spirit. Nor is this all. As he has sinned against God, so he has also sinned against his neighbor. The fifth tells him of his stubbornness and disobedience. The sixth, of his passions, and desires of revenge. The seventh, of his lewdness. The eighth, of his covetous thefts. The ninth, of his lies and slanders, backbitings, and rash judgment. The tenth, of his covetous thoughts, and motions of the heart to all manner of evil. Good Lord! What a number of evils, yes, what innumerable swarms of *lawless thoughts*, and *words*, and *actions* does he read in his conscience? But above all, his beloved sin is written in the greatest and largest characters. This he finds to have bewitched him most, and to have domineered above all the rest in his wasted conscience. It is there that he may read it, together with his other sins. So the Spirit of God now opens the eyes of his mind, and lets him see the very mud and filth of his soul that lays at the bottom which before was unseen, and undiscerned. This is the first working of the new life, in other words, a feeling of the old death of his soul in sins and trespasses. And here the axiom is true, *no generation without corruption*; a man must first *feel* this death, before he is born again.

Step Two

The second step is a sense of divine wrath, which begets in him fear. No sooner has the man a sight and feeling of his sin, now called the Spirit of bondage, but then God's Spirit presents to him the armory of God's flaming wrath and fiery indignation. This makes him to feel, as if he were pricked with the stroke of an arrow, or point of a sword, or sting of an adder, that he is a most accursed and damnable creature, justly deserving all the miseries of this life, and all the torments of hell in that life to come; yes, this makes him tremble, and stand, and look, as if he were thoroughly frightened with the angry countenance of God Almighty. Would you view him in this case? His conscience has now awakened him out of his dead sleep, by the trumpet of the Law. His heart is now scorched with the secret sense of God's angry face. His soul is now full sorely crushed under the most grievous burden of innumerable sins. His thoughts are now full of fear and astonishment, as if no less than very hell and horror were ready to seize on his body and soul. I do not say what measure of this wrath is poured on all men, for I suppose some feel more and some less. But I truly believe, there are some that (in these pangs of the new birth), have been scorched as it were, with the very flames of hell. And no wonder, for this is the time of fear. It is now that Satan strives busily to stifle the new man in the womb; and therefore he that before diminished his sins, and made them appear little in his eyes, when he once sees the man smitten down into the place of dragons, and covered with the shadow of death, then he puts into his mind his innumerable sins, and, that which immediately follows, the curse of the law, and the wrath of God. He makes this more grisly and fierce, with a purpose to plunge him into the abyss of horror and despair. By this means he persuaded Cain to cry out "My iniquity is greater than can be forgiven," (Gen. 4:13). The unregenerate only goes so far with the man born again; both have a sight of sin, and sense of wrath, but here they part. The unregenerate man either sinks under it, or labors to allay it with worldly comforts. But the man that is born again seeks the right way to cure it, and at last, by the help of God's Spirit, he passes quite through it. I mean through this hell upon earth, into the spiritual pleasures of the kingdom of grace, which is to be born again.

The Third Step

The third step is *sorrow for sin*, and this is more peculiar to God's child. His heart grieves, his eye weeps; the way to God's kingdom is to cry like children coming into the world; the way to be new born is to feel as a woman laboring with child, and so Christ is *formed in us*. Can a man be born again without bitterness of soul? No, if he ever comes to a sight of sin, and God's sanctifying Spirit works in him sorrow for sin, his soul will mourn. It is true, some infants are born with more pain, and some with less: but more or less.; it cannot be so little, but the man that labors in these pangs shall mourn.

THE FOURTH STEP

The fourth step is *seeking rightly for comfort*. He does not run to the world, or flesh, or devil, who are miserable comforters. Instead he runs to scripture, to prayer, or to the ministry of God's word. If he finds comfort in the scriptures, he meets with it in the Gospel. And if it pleases God that the man, now laboring in his pangs of the new birth, does rightly settle his thoughts on the Gospel of Christ, no doubt there he may suck the sweetest comforts that ever were revealed to man. Or if he finds comfort in prayer, to which he ever and later walks in every step there, then he knows it is all by Christ by whose name he approaches to that throne of grace. No sooner had the king of Nineveh humbled himself, but his proclamation runs this way, "Let man and beast be covered with sackcloth, and cry mightily unto God. Who can tell if God will turn and repent, and turn away from his fierce anger, that we perish not?" Why? "For word came unto the king of Nineveh, and he arose from his throne, and he laid his robe from him, and covered him with sackcloth, and sat in ashes," (Jonah 3:6). And so the man now wrestling with grievous terrors of conscience, who can tell, he thinks to himself, if God will turn away his fierce anger? Let me then cry mightily to the Lord of heaven; let me cry, and continue crying until the Lord of mercy looks on me. And if for all this God gives him a repulse, for reasons best known to himself, if at the first, second, third, fourth, or at many more times, he seems to have cried in vain, at last he flies to the ministry of the word, and if he may have his will, he would hit on the most soul-searching man among God's messengers. At last he comes to God's minister, with a what shall I do, what must I do to be saved? Alas! now I feel the wounded conscience, the broken heart, the spiritual blindness, the captivity and poverty, of which often you have told me. If then there is any instruction, direction or duty, which may tend to my good, now direct me in God's fear, and I will willingly follow it with my utmost endeavors.

And now, and not until now, has God's minister a strong and seasonable call to magnify the sufficiency of Christ's death and passion. If the blood of Christ, and promise of salvation proffered to an unwounded conscience, as it were, but like the pouring of a sovereign balsam on a sound member of man, such is the only right everlasting method that God uses to convert sinners. First to wound by the Law, and then to heal by the Gospel. First to cause pain for sin, and then to lay to a medicine of Christ's blood. And therefore when the heart is broken, then the man of God has his warrant to bind it up again. Then may he magnify God's mercy. Then may he set out to the height of the beauty of Christ's passion and person, and in this way by his high and holy art of comforting the afflicted, at last the child of God, prepared for his birth, is born again.

The Fifth Step

The fifth step is a clear, I do not say a general sight which he had before, but the clear sight of Christ laid open to the eye of faith; no sooner is the poor wounded soul informed thoroughly in the mystery and mercy of the gospel, but he then looks on his Savior as the Jews on the brazen serpent, and seeing him lifted upon the cross, he cannot but see in him an infinite treasure of mercy and love; a boundless and bottomless sea of tender-heartedness and pity, a whole heaven of sweetness, happiness, peace and pleasures. After the spirit of bondage, enters the Spirit of adoption. The terrors of the Law lead him to the comforts of the Gospel. His sorrow for sin brings him to the clear light of his Savior, and then as a man in death-pangs, that lifts up his eyes to heaven, where his help comes from, so he in birth-pangs lifts up his eyes to Christ, who must either help him, or he sinks under his. These sins will sink him to the bottom of hell if Christ does not rescue him. And this sight of Christ Jesus to an humbled sinner, together with those glorious privileges which he brings with him, is a most pleasant, ravishing, heavenly sight. Not all the curious sights on earth, nor all those glittering spangles in heaven, can possibly afford such pleasure to the eye of man, as does this one object of Christ bleeding on the cross, to the soul of a sinner. Imagine you saw some malefactor led to the place of execution; if this man should suddenly see his king running towards him with his pardon in his hand, what a sight would this be? So it is with the man sorrowing for sin; while he is weeping his case, and confessing what a little step there is between him and damnation, in amazement he looks on Christ, whom he sees with a spear in his side, with thorns on his head, with nails in his feet, with a pardon in his hands, offering it to all men, that will but receive it by faith. O! here is a sight indeed, able to revive the most wicked man on earth, dead in sins and trespasses. And now there is hope of the birth. We may call this the *stirrings* of God's child, or the *first feelings* of life, before he is born again.

The Sixth Step

The sixth step is a *hungering desire after Christ and his merits.* O here is a thirst above all thirsts! It breeds ardent desires, vehement longings, unutterable groans, mighty gaspings, just like the dry and thirsty ground that gasps and cleaves, and opens for drops of rain. This is that violent affection that God puts into the hearts of those who seek him in sincerity and truth; never was Ahab more sick for a vineyard, nor Sisera for milk, nor Samson for water, than is a truly humbled soul after Christ; ever thirsting and longing, that he may hide himself in that blood which his Savior shed for him. I have read of a gracious woman, who laboring in these pangs, and longing after Christ Jesus, cried out, *I have borne nine children with as great pain as other women, and yet I would with all my heart bear them all over again, yes, bear them all the days of my life, to be assured of my part in Christ Jesus.* One replying, does not your heart desire and long after him? *Oh* (she said), *I have an husband and children, and many other comforts, I would give them all, and all the good I shall ever see in this world, or in the world to come, to have my poor thirsty soul refreshed with that precious blood of my Savior.* So eager and earnest is the heart of each man (parched with the angry countenance of God), after his blood; I thirst, I faint, I languish, I long, (he says), for one drop of mercy; my spirit is melted in me into tears of blood; my heart, because of sin, is so shaken and shivered; my soul, because of sorrow, is so wasted and parched, that my thirst is insatiable, my bowels are hot within me after Christ. All these expressions are far short of those longings; no man knows them, except him that receives them, except the one who is born again.

THE SEVENTH STEP

The seventh step is *a relying on Christ*. A man considers those invitations of our Lord and Savior: "If any man thirst, let him come unto me." "Ho, every one that thirsteth, come ye to the waters," "Come unto me all ye that are weary and heavy laden." But (resting himself on these blessed promises), he throws himself into the merciful arms of his crucified Lord. Come life, come death, come heaven, come hell, come what will, here will he stick forever. Paul says, "Who shall separate us from the love of Christ? shall tribulation, or distress, or persecution, or famine, or nakedness, or peril, or sword? As it is written, For thy sake we are killed all the day long; we are accounted as sheep for the slaughter. Nay, in all these things we are more than conquerors through him that loved us. For I am persuaded, that neither death, nor life, nor angels, nor principalities, nor powers, nor things present, nor things to come, Nor height, nor depth, nor any other creature, shall be able to separate us from the love of God, which is in Christ Jesus our Lord," (Rom 8:35-39). So it is with the man laboring in this birth. What? (he says), does Christ call the heavy-laden? Why, Lord, I am heavy-laden with a weight, a mass of sin. And if he may come that is called, Lord, I come, I come, and now I come, with thee will I build my tabernacle, with thee will I rest for ever. This affiance, dependence, reliance, (or whatsoever else we call it), on the *merits of Christ*, is the right justifying faith. Now, no matter if a man *once* comes, there is but *one degree more*, and he is then born again.

The Eight and Last Step

The last and highest step is *universal obedience to Christ*. No sooner has he cast himself on him, but he takes him (not only as a Savior to redeem him from the miseries of sin, but), as an husband, a Lord, a King to serve him, love him, honor him, and obey him. Now will he take his yoke on him; now will he bear his cross, and follow him; now will he walk in the holy path; now will he associate himself to that sect that is everywhere spoken against; now will he oppose himself against all sin whatsoever; now will he shake off his old companions, brethren in iniquity. New, he will keep peace and a good conscience towards God and man. Now will he watch over his secret sins, and all occasions of evil; now he will direct his words to the glorifying of God, and to give grace to the hearers. Now he will conform all his actions to the sovereignty of grace. Now he will delight in the word, the Gospel ways, the saints, the services of God. He will sell all, all that he has, even all his sins, down to the last filthy rag of his beloved bosom-sin. And "now old things are passed away, behold all things are become new," (2 Cor. 5: 17). His heart, his eye, his ear, his tongue, his understandings his will, his memory, his conscience, his love, his hatred, his hope, his fear, his joy, his sorrow; will *you* give any more? His thoughts, his words, his actions, his affections, are all *new*; this conversion is *universal*, this change is a *thorough* change. Now Christ is formed in him and now he is transformed into a new creature. He is made new. God the Father accepts him for his Son, God the Son stamps on him the image of his Father, but more immediately, God the Holy Spirit has in this way molded and fashioned him, as I have let you see him, and now he is born again, which...except a man be, he (*shall not*), cannot see the kingdom of God.

So here are those steps that raise up man to the state of regeneration, a sight of sin, sense of misery, sorrow for sin, seeking for comfort, a sight of Christ, desire after Christ, relying on Christ, obedience to Christ. However, I have one word more before we have finished this part.

Discerning Being Born Again

You see how God brings along the man whom he purposes to make his; and yet let no truly humbled sinner be discouraged if he does not observe so distinctly the order of these steps, and especially in that degree as we have related; for if in substance and effect they have been worked, if he has them in truth, (though perhaps not in this degree), I dare pronounce, that he is *surely* born again. It is one of our worthies who *said*,

> In our humiliations, and other preparative dispositions, we do not prescribe precisely just such a measure and quantity, we do not determine peremptorily upon such or such a degree and height, we leave that to the wisdom of our great Master in heaven. But sure we are, a man must have so much, and in that measure, as thoroughly to humble him, and then to bring him to his Savior; he must be weary of all his sins, and of Satan's bondage wholly, willing to pluck out his right eye, and cut off his right hand; I mean to part with his beloved bosom lusts, to sell all, and not to leave so much as an hoof behind: he must see his danger, and so haste to the city of refuge; he must be sensible of his spiritual misery, that he may heartily thirst for mercy; he must find himself lost that Christ may be all in all unto him; and after must follow an hatred of all false and evil ways for the time to come, a thorough change of former courses, company,

conversation, and setting himself in the practice of sobriety, honesty, and holiness.

And another *speaks*,

> That the discovery of the remedy as soon as the misery must necessarily prevent a great part of the trouble, and make the distinct effects on the soul to be with much more difficulty discerned: no, the acts of the soul are so quick, and often so confused, that the distinct orders of these workings may not be apprehended, or remembered. And perhaps the joyful apprehension of mercy may make the sense of misery sooner forgotten."

The sum is that of every soul this much is required: first, a truly penitent sight, sense, and hatred of all sin. Secondly, a sincere and insatiable thirst after Jesus Christ, and his righteousness, both imputed and inherent. Thirdly, an unfeigned, and unreserved resolution of an universal new obedience for the time to come. If any man has had the experience of these affections and effects in his own soul, whatsoever the order, or whatsoever the measure is, he may go on comfortably in the holy faith.

Now then let me advise thee (whosoever you are that reads), to enter into your own soul and examine your own state, whether or not you are yet born again? Search and see, whether as yet the spirit of bondage has worked its effects in you. See and examine whether you have been enlightened, convinced, and terrified with a sensible apprehension, and particular acknowledgment of your wretched estate? Search and see, whether as yet the Spirit of adoption has sealed you for his own; whether (after your heart being broken, your spirit bruised, your soul humbled, your conscience wounded and awaked), you have had a sight of Christ, and have thirsted after him, and have followed his ways and commandments by a universal obedience? If upon searching this out you can say (without self-deceit), that it is so with you, then you may bless God that ever you were born; certainly (I dare say it), *you are born again*. But if *not*, if all I have spoken is very mysterious to you, what shall I say? If you ever mean to see the kingdom of God, strive, endeavor with all your might to become truly regenerate. You may say, perhaps it is not in your power. Who can command the Spirit of the Lord, that blows where he wishes? I answer, it is *indeed* the Spirit, and not man, that regenerates or sanctifies. But I answer with this, the doctrine of the Gospel is the ministration of the Spirit, and wherever that is preached (as I preach it now to you), there the Holy Spirit is present, and there he comes to be regenerate. If then as yet you do not feel this mighty work of God in you, and yet you might not feel it. I shall lend you two wings to bear you, two hands to lead you to the foot of the ladder, where if you ascend these steps aforesaid, I dare pronounce that you are born again.

Two Wings of Help

The first wing is *prayer*, which first brings you to God's throne, and then to the new birth. "Take with you words, and turn to the LORD: say unto him, Take away all iniquity, and receive us graciously: so will we render the calves of our lips," (Hosea 14:2). And then it follows, "I will heal their backsliding, I will love them freely." The soul may object, I may say this, and be no better. But I answer, say it, though you are no better because God bids you to say it. Say it, and say it again, and again. It may be that he will come in when you say it. The soul may object again, how can I pray, and not have faith? I answer, put yourself on prayer, and who knows, a blessing and true faith may come. It is *the Lord* that converts and heals, and saves; and prayer is the means to produce this effect in you. When we are required to pray, to repent and believe, we are not to seek strength in ourselves, but to search into the Covenant of Grace in Christ, and turn the *promise* into *prayer*. Therefore, bow your knees, and humbly, and heartily, frequently, and fervently implore the influence of God's blessed Spirit. Would you ask, and continue asking? Would you cry, and continue crying? Then I could assure you of the promise which God has made, and cannot deny. "He that asketh receiveth; and he that seeketh findeth, and to him that knocketh (*by continuance and perseverance*), it shall be opened," (Matt. 7:8).

The second wing that bears you to these steps of the new birth is *constant hearing of the word.* You must attend the gates of wisdom, and wait at her posts. You must come to God's house, and hearken to the ministry of the word, and you shall see at one time or another that God will remember you in mercy. It is true, I do not know when, and therefore I wish you not to miss a day to repair to God's house, unless the day of your neglect might have been the day of your conversion. It is certain, no man should expect God's blessing without his ordinances; there is no eating of bread without ploughing and sowing, no recovering of health without eating and drinking. So, in the same way, there is no blessing, no grace, no regeneration, without waiting on God in his ways, and in his ordinances. Now then, as you desire heaven or (the way to heaven), to be born again, I beseech you: *make high account of this ordinance of God.* In preaching the Gospel, light, motion and power go out to all who hear, which *men resist.* And some are destroyed, not because they could not believe, but because they *resist*, and will not obey, so they die, (*cf*. Acts 7:11ff). (See also Luke 13:34; Ezek. 33:11. Hos. 13:9). And yet I wish that you not only hear it, but after you have heard it, consider it, ponder on it; and lay the threats and reproofs, the precepts and promises, to your own soul. So if you hear and meditate, I do not doubt but God's word will be a word of power to you, and (together with prayer), bring you towards the new birth, for except a man comes, *he cannot see the kingdom of God*.

Righteousness, Peace and Joy in the Holy Spirit

To see, is all one as to enjoy: yet a man may see that which he does not enjoy: but without regeneration there is no sight, much less possession of the kingdom of God.

If by the kingdom of God is meant the kingdom of grace, (of which our Savior speaks, "the kingdom of God is within you," Luke 17:21), see to what a privilege the new man has attained. All the graces of God, all the fruits of the Spirit are now poured into him. If you ask, what graces? What fruits? Paul tells you, Gal. 5:22, "Love, Joy, Peace, Long-suffering, Gentleness, Goodness, Faith, Meekness, Temperance," or would you have us to contract them? Paul does it elsewhere, "The kingdom of God is...righteousness, peace, and joy in the Holy Spirit," (Rom. 16:17).

First, *righteousness.* No sooner is a man born again, but he enters into the holy path, he declines all evil, and stands at the sword's point with his beloved sin. Or if ever any sin (through the violence of temptation), seizes on him again, he is presently put again into the pangs of the new birth, and so renewing his sorrow, and repairing repentance, he becomes more resolute and watchful over all his ways. And as he abhors evil, so he cleaves to that which is good. His faith, like the sun, sets all those heavenly stars in shining hope, and love, and zeal, and humility, and patience; in a word, universal obedience, and fruitfulness in all good works, not one, but all good duties of the first and second table, begin to be natural and familiar to him.

Secondly, no sooner is a man righteous, but he is at peace with man, at peace with God, at peace with himself. He is at peace with man, "The wolf also shall dwell with the lamb, and the leopard shall lie down with the kid; and the calf and the young lion and the fatling together; and a little child shall lead them," (Isa. 11:6). The meaning is that in the kingdom of Christ, when a man is called into the state of grace (however by nature he is a wolf, or a leopard, or a lion, or a bear, yet), he shall then lay aside his cruelty, and live peaceably with all men. He is at peace with God, he has humbled himself, and confessed his fault and cried for mercy, and cast himself on Christ. So now God, by his word, has spoken peace to his soul. By the mediation of Christ it is obtained, and by the testimony of the Spirit he feels it within him. This is that peace which passes all understanding. It made the angels sing *peace on earth*; it makes his soul reply, *my peace is in heaven*. He is at peace with himself, I mean his own conscience; that which before stirred up the fire, that brought him to a sight of sin, and sense of divine wrath, that filled him with fearful terrors, remorse and sorrow, is now quiet. Solomon calls it a *continual feast*, (Prov. 15:15). Who are the attendants, but the holy angels? Where is the most cheer but joy in the Holy Spirit? Who is the feast-maker, but God himself, and his good Spirit dwelling in him? Nor is this feast without music. God's word, and his actions, make a blessed harmony, and he endeavors to continue it by keeping, peace, and a good conscience towards God and man.

Thirdly, from this peace issues joy in the Holy Spirit. No sooner is a man at peace with man, with God, with himself, but he is filled with joy that no man can take from him; this joy I take to be those blessed stirrings of the heart, when the seal of remission of sins is first set unto the soul by the spirit of adoption. For so it is, the soul having newly passed the pangs of the new birth, it is presently bathed in the blood of Christ, lulled in the bosom of God's mercies, secured by the Spirit of its inheritance, and so ordinary follows a sea of comfort, a sensible taste of everlasting pleasures.

If by the kingdom of God is meant the kingdom of glory, see then what a privilege waits on the new man; no sooner shall his breath and body be divorced, but his soul, mounted on the wings of angels, shall be carried straight above the starry firmament, there to inherit the kingdom of God surely called so, for it is a kingdom of God's own making, beautifying, and blessing. It is a kingdom demonstrating the glorious residence of the King of kings. But here my discourse must give way to your meditation. In this fountain of pleasure, let the new-born Christian bathe his soul. For it is his, and it is only he that shall see it, enjoy it. "Except a man be born again, no man shall ever see the kingdom of God."

So we have the privileges of the new birth. There faith waits on it, and righteousness, and peace, and joy in the Holy Spirit; in a word, the kingdom of grace, and the kingdom of glory.

PART 2: THE DOCTRINE OF REGENERATION EXPLAINED FURTHER

SECTION 1: THE OCCASION AND METHOD OF THIS PART OF THE TREATISE.

There are some who, hearing the new birth to be so necessary to salvation, but never feeling in themselves any such change, have desired further helps. I advised them in the former treatise to be frequent in prayer, and hearing of the word. But so we have done (they say), and yet we feel no conversion. It may be so, for not always the doing of them, but perseverance in them through Christ obtains the blessing. I shall, for their further satisfaction, give them a more particular method.

Two things are necessary for them that would have part in the new birth: 1. To get into it. 2. To be delivered of it.

1. The means to get into it, are, 1. An examination of themselves. 2. Confession of their sins. 3. Hearty prayer for the

softening of their hearts. By which are obtained the three first steps; *sight of sin, sense of divine wrath, sorrow for sin* as already said.

2. The means to be delivered out, is by application of the promises; and these produce their several effects; as, a sight of Christ; a desire after Christ; a relying on Christ; and obedience to Christ.

SECTION 2: THE FIRST MEANS TO GET INTO THE NEW BIRTH

I. The means to get into the new birth, is, first, *examination*. And the way to examine is to set before men that crystal-glass of the Law for their light and rule. To this purpose I have here annexed a catalogue; not that I can possibly enumerate all sins, but only the kinds; and if in this I come short, yet conscience may by it bring into their thoughts those others not mentioned.

Now then (whosoever you are that begin this blessed work), examine yourself by this catalogue, but do it warily, and truly; and where you find yourself, either note it in this book, or transcribe it into some paper, so that they may be ready for you when you come to confession.

II. Sins against the First Commandment

In every commandment we must observe both the duties required, and sins forbidden, for both of these are implied in every one of the commandments; if in the first you are guilty, you must answer negatively; if in the second, you must answer affirmatively.

Now then to proceed: *Thou shalt have no other gods but me.*

For the Duties Required

Say, first, have you ever taken the true God in Christ to be your God? Secondly, have you abounded in those graces by which you should cleave to God, as in knowledge and love, and fear, and joy, and trusting in God? Thirdly, have you observed God's mercies, and promises, and works, and judgments on you, and (by a particular application), took special notice of them? Fourthly, have you communicated with the godly, and joined yourself to God's people, and delighted chiefly in them.

For the Sins Forbidden

Say, first, have you not sometimes been guilty of blasphemy, or idolatry, or witchcraft, or atheism? Secondly, have you not been guilty of pride, a sin flatly opposing God, and first committed by devils? Thirdly, do you not have some inward reasonings that there is no God, or that he does not see, or does not know, or that there is no profit in his service?

Fifthly, have you not trusted in man, or feared man, or loved the world, and by this alienated your heart from God. Sixthly, have you not resorted to witches, or in the first place to physicians, and not to the living God? Seventhly, have you not tempted God, and in the matters of God, been either cold, or luke-warm, or preposterously zealous? Eighthly, have you not been careless to perform the inward duties of God's worship in sincerity and truth? If in those you have transgressed, then you have broken this commandment!

III. Sins against the Second Commandment

Thou shalt not make to thyself any Graven Image.

For the Duties Required

Say, first, have you ever worshipped the true God purely according to his will? Secondly, have you observed all those outward duties of his worship, as prayer, and vows, and fasting, and meditation, and the rest? Thirdly, have you repaired to God's house, observed family duties, received the preachers of the gospel?

For the Sins Forbidden

Say, first, have you not sometimes walked after the imaginations of your own heart, serving God out of custom? Secondly, have you not committed idol worship, conceiving of God in your mind in the likeness of a creature? Thirdly, have you not made an image to look like God, or used any gesture of love and reverence to any such images? Have you not been careless to worship God, to call on the Lord, to receive God's ministers, or to perform any other of the outward duties of God's worship? If in any of these you have transgressed, then have you broken this commandment.

IV. SINS AGAINST THE THIRD COMMANDMENT

Thou shall not take the Name of the Lord thy God in vain.

For the Duties Required

Say, first, have you been a constant learner, hearer, and doer of God's word and will? Secondly, have you prayed with perseverance, understanding, and power of the spirit, without doubting or wavering? Thirdly, have you come preparedly to the sacrament of the Lord's supper, and having come, have you discerned the Lord's body? Fourthly, have you used all the titles and properties, and works, and ordinances of the Lord with knowledge, faith, reverence, joy and sincerity,

For the Sins Forbidden

Say, first, have you not sometimes, in your talk dishonored the titles, attributes, religion, word, people of God, or anything that has in it the print of his holiness? Secondly, have you not caused the name of religion, or people of God to be ill thought of by your ill course of life? Thirdly, have you not rashly, or unpreparedly, or heedlessly, read the word, heard sermons, received the sacraments, or performed any other part of the worship of God? Fourthly, have you not thought or spoken blasphemously, or contemptuously of God, or of anything whatsoever pertaining to God? If in any of these you have transgressed, then have you broken this commandment.

V. SINS AGAINST THE FOURTH COMMANDMENT

Remember thou keep Holy the Sabbath Day.

For the Duties Required

Say, first, have you (according to the equity of this commandment,), ever observed the Lord's Day, and other days and times set apart for God's service? Secondly, have you always prepared your heart, before you went into the house of the Lord, by meditation of God's words and works, by examination and reformation of your ways, by prayer, thanksgiving, and holy resolution to carry yourself as in God's presence, and to hear and obey whatsoever you should learn out of the pure word of God? Have you repaired to God's house in due time, and stayed the whole time of prayer, reading, preaching of the word, singing of psalms, receiving the sacraments? Have you performed private religious offices on the Lord's Day in private prayer and thanksgiving, in acknowledging your offences to God, in reconciling yourself to those you have offended, or with whom you are at variance; in visiting the sick, comforting the afflicted, contributing to the necessity of the poor, instructing your children and servants (and the rest of your family), in the fear and nurture of the Lord?

For the Sins Forbidden

Say, first, have you not sometimes spent the Lord's Day in idleness, or in worldly business, in vanities, or in sin? Secondly, have you not omitted public duties, or come in too late, or went out too soon? Thirdly, have you not employed your cattle, or servants, or children, or any other, though you did not work yourself? Have you not profaned the Lord's Day by needless works, words, or thoughts about your calling, or about your recreation? Have the strict observance of the duties of that day been tedious to you, saying in your heart, *when will the day be gone*? If in any of these you have transgressed, then have you broken this commandment.

VI. SINS AGAINST THE FIFTH COMMANDMENT

Honor thy Father and thy Mother.

For the duties here required: they are either in the family, common-wealth, or church.

First, for the family: Say, if you are a husband: 1. Have you loved your wife, and dealt with her according to knowledge, giving honor to her as the weaker vessel, and as being heirs together of the grace of life, that your prayers were not hindered? If you are a wife: 2. Have you submitted to your own husband, as to the Lord in everything? 3. Have you put on the ornament of a meek and quiet spirit? If you are a parent: 4. Have you brought up your children in the nurture and admonition of the Lord? 5. Have you corrected them, yet not provoked them by immoderate correction? 6. Have you provided for them in their callings, or outward estates? If you are a child: 7. Have you obeyed your parents, and received correction with submission and reverence? 8. Have you relieved them in their lack? 9. Have you observed their instructions, and covered their infirmities? If you are a master: 10. Have you entertained God's servants, and given to your servant that which is just and equal? If you are a servant: 11. Have you been obedient to your master according to the flesh, with fear and trembling, in singleness of heart, as to Christ?

Not answering again, nor purloining, but showing all good fidelity.

Secondly, for the common-wealth; if you are a magistrate: 12. Have you executed just laws? 13. Have you reformed others abuses, according to the power that is in you? If you are a subject: 14. Have you obeyed the higher powers in all just commands? 15. Have you been subject to them, not only for wrath, but also for conscience's sake.

Thirdly, for the church; if you are a minister: 16. Have you taught in season, and out of season? 17. Has your light shined before men, that they might see your good works? If you are a hearer: 18. Have you communicated to them that teach you in all good things? 19. Have you obeyed them, and prayed for them, and loved them, and followed them, considering the end of their conversation?

For the Sins Forbidden

And first, for the family: say, if you are an husband: 1. Have you not sometimes abused your wife, or injured her in thought, word, or deed? If you are a wife: 2. Have you not been wasteful, or froward, or idle? If you are a parent: 3. Have you not been careless, especially of your children's souls? If you are a child: 4. Have you not despised your father's or mother's instructions? 5. Have you not mocked them, or shamed them, or grieved them? If you are a master: 6. Have you not governed your family negligently? 7. Have you not with-held that which is just and equal in diet, wages and encouragement? If you are a servant: Have you not been idle and slothful? 9. Have you not served grudgingly, and not from the heart?

Secondly, for the common-wealth: if you are a magistrate; 10. Have you not been as a lion, or a bear, roaring and raging against the poor people? 11. Have you not decreed unrighteous decrees? Respecting the persons of the poor, or honoring the persons of the mighty? If you are a subject: 12. Have you not reviled the *gods* (i.e. magistrates that God has set up over you), or cursed the rulers of your people? 13. Have you not disobeyed the higher powers, or denied tribute, or custom, or honor, or fear, to whom they are due?

Thirdly, for the church: If you are a minister; 14. Have you not been profane in your life and conversation? 15. Have you not run before you were sent? Or being sent, have you not been negligent in the gift that is in you? 16. Have you not caused God's people to err? 17. Have you not committed simony, or sought indirectly for the fleece, not regarding the flock? 18. Have you not strengthened the hands of evil doers, in preaching peace to wicked men? 19. Have you not given heed to fables (or to some unprofitable matter), rather than godly edifying which is in faith? If you are a hearer: 20. Have you not resisted the minister, and the word preached by him?

Whatsoever you are, husband, or wife, or parent, or child, or master, or servant, or magistrate, or subject, or minister, or hearer, if in any of these you have transgressed, then have you broken this commandment.

VII. SINS AGAINST THE SIXTH COMMANDMENT

Thou shalt do no murder.

FOR THE DUTIES REQUIRED

Say, first, have you ever desired and studied by all lawful means, to preserve your own person, and the person of your neighbor?

FOR THE SINS FORBIDDEN

Say, first, have you not sometimes envied others? Secondly, have you not offended others in words, by censuring, or reviling-, or rendering evil for evil, or railing for railing? Thirdly, have you not offended others in deeds, plotting against the just, or doing evil to any man? Fourthly, have you not been angry with your brother without cause, or continued long in anger? Fifthly, have you not rejoiced at others fall? Or wished a curse to their souls? Sixthly, have you not done evil to yourself, by inordinate fretting, or grieving, or drinking, or saying in your passions *would to God I were dead*? Seventhly, have you not been a sower of discord, or some way or other, an occasion of discomfort, or of the death of your neighbor? If in any of these you have transgressed, you have then broken this commandment.

VIII. SINS AGAINST THE SEVENTH COMMANDMENT

Thou shall not commit adultery.

For the Duties Required

Say, have you ever kept yourself pure in soul and body, both towards yourself and others.

For the Sins Forbidden

Say, have you not sometimes been defiled with whoredom, adultery, polygamy, or self-pollution? Secondly, have you not offended in the occasions of uncleanness, as in idleness, gluttony, drunkenness, wanton company, or gay attire? Thirdly, have you not sinned in your senses, or gestures, or words? Fourthly, have you not harbored in your heart impure thoughts, inordinate affections? Fifthly, have you not behaved yourself immodestly, using some manner of dalliance and wantonness? If in any of these you have transgressed, then have you broken this commandment.

IX. SINS AGAINST THE EIGHTH COMMANDMENT

Thou shalt not steal.

For the Duties Required.

Say, have you by all good means, furthered the outward estate of yourself and of your neighbor?

For the Sins Forbidden

Say first, have you not sometimes obtained your living by an unlawful calling? Secondly, have you not impoverished yourself by idleness, or unnecessary expenses? Thirdly, have you not with-held from yourself, or others, that which should have been expended? Fourthly, have you not gotten, or kept your neighbor's goods by falsehood or force, and made no restitution? Fifthly, have you not stolen; by usury, or oppression, or fraud in buying or selling? Sixthly, have you not robbed God of his tithes and offerings? Seventhly, have you not in some way or other impaired your neighbor's estate? If in any of these you have transgressed, then have you broken this commandment.

X. SINS AGAINST THE NINTH COMMANDMENT

Thou shalt not bear false witness.

For the Duties Required

Say, have you ever by all means sought to maintain your own and your neighbor's good name, according to truth and a good conscience?

For the Sins Forbidden

Say, first, have you not sometimes loved (or made), a lie? Secondly, have you not raised a false report? Thirdly, have you not censured or judged others? Fourthly, have you not flattered yourself and others, saying to the wicked, you are righteous? Fifthly, have you not condemned some? Without witness, or forborn to witness for others when you knew the truth? Sixthly, have you not been uncharitably suspicious or a despiser of your neighbor? Seventhly, have you not told a lie, whether jestingly, or officiously, or perniciously? If in any of these you have transgressed, then have you broken this commandment.

XI. SINS AGAINST THE LAST COMMANDMENT

Thou shalt not covet.

For the Duties Required.

Say, first, have you ever been truly contented with your own outward condition? Secondly, have you rejoiced at others good, and loved your neighbor as yourself?

For the Sins Forbidden

Say, first, have you not sometimes conceived evil thoughts in your heart? Secondly, have you not been discontented with your own condition? Have you not coveted after something or other that was your neighbor's? If in any of these you have transgressed, then have you broken this commandment.

Section 3: The second Means to get into the New Birth: Confession

After examination, (which may serve you for one day's work or two), the next duty is *confession*. Take a catalogue of those sins which you have noted, and spread your catalogue before the Lord; there read seriously, and particularly, saying, *O Lord, I confess I have committed this sin, and the other sin* (as they are in order), *of all these sins I am guilty, especially of those sins in which I delighted, my darlings, my bosom-sins,* (take notice of them and confess them again), *of all these sins I am guilty; and now, O Lord, standing, as it were, at the bar of your tribunal, I arraign myself, and accuse myself, and judge myself worthy of the utmost of your wrath and indignation. For one sin you cast Adam out of paradise, for one sin you cast the angels out of heaven, and what then shall become of me, that have committed a world of sins?*—(Here pause a while, and meditate on your unworthiness), *O that I should be so foolish, so brutish, so mad, to commit these sins, these manifold sins! O that by these sins I should break so holy a law, provoke so good and great a majesty! What should I do, but remembering my evil ways, even loathe myself in my own sight* (yes *abhor myself in dust and ashes*), for my iniquities and my abominations?

For conclusion, you may imitate the publican, who not daring to lift up his eyes, struck his chest: so do yourself, and say with him, *God be merciful to me a sinner.*

Section 4: The third Means to get into the New Birth.

After confession (which may well serve you for another day's work), seek for true sorrow and mourning for your sins. You must seek, and never leave seeking, until you feel your heart melt within you. To this purpose read some tracts of death, of judgment, of hell, of Christ's passion, of the joys of heaven. Last of all (and I take it best of all), resolve to set some time apart every day to beg it of the Lord: and at the time appointed, fall down on your knees, spread your catalogue of sins out, confess, accuse, judge, condemn yourself again; beg of the Lord to give you that soft heart he promised, "A new heart also will I give you, and a new spirit will I put within you: and I will take away the stony heart out of your flesh, and I will give you an heart of flesh," (Ezek. 36:26). Then say to yourself, is this the Lord's promise? O Lord perform it to my heart; take away my stony heart, and give me a heart of flesh, a new heart, a new spirit, *etc.*— (Here make your own prayer: do not be careful of words, only let the words be the true voice of your heart.), Pray, and call and cry with vehemence and fervency not to be uttered. When you have done, if the Lord does not yet hear you, pray again the next day, and the next day, yes, put on this resolution, that you will never leave off praying until the Lord hears you in mercy, until he makes you to feel your heart melt within you. Yes, (if it may be), until you see your tears trickling you are your cheeks, because of your offences. The Lord will, perhaps, hear your at the first time, or at the second time, or if he does not, do not be discouraged, God has his times. God speaks once and twice, and a man does not perceive what he says. Happy is he who relents at last. Do not give it over, but instead persist, your suit is just, and importunity will prevail.

2. The first Reason for this Sorrow.

This must be done; first, because "without pangs there is no birth." The pangs of a penitent man are as the pangs of a woman. Now, as there can be no birth without pains of travail going before, so neither can there be true repentance without some terrors of the law, and straits of conscience. *You have not received the spirit of bondage again to fear*, the apostle says to the Romans, to show us they once did receive it. When? But in the very first preparation to conversion; it was then that the Spirit of God in the Law did so bear witness to them of their bondage, "that it made them to fear." And certainly it was this way with every man in his first conversion. His contrition must be vehement, bruising, breaking, renting the heart, and feeling the pains (as a woman laboring of child), before there can be a new birth.

3. The second Reason for this Sorrow.

Again, without contrition, there is no Christ; therefore it was John Baptist (Chrysostom says), who "first thoroughly frightened the minds of his hearers with the terror of judgment, and expectation of torment, and when he had in this way taken down the stubbornness, then at length he makes mention of Christ." Certainly, the first thing that draws to Christ, is to consider our miserable estate without him; no man will come to Christ except he is hungry; no man will take Christ's yoke upon him, until he comes to know the weight of Satan's yoke. To this end, therefore must every man be broken with lashes of conscience, that so despairing of himself he may fly to Christ.

4. The Third Reason for this Sorrow.

Again, without hearty sorrow, no spiritual comfort can come to us. We must first be humbled before the Lord, and *then* he will lift us up. God does not pour the oil of his mercy except into a broken vessel. God never comforts thoroughly, except where he finds humiliation and repentance for sin. "The word of God," one *says*,

> ...has three degrees of operation in the hearts of his chosen; first, it falls to men's ears as the sound of many waters, a mighty, a great and confused sound, and which commonly brings neither terror nor joy, but a wondering and acknowledgment of a strange force; this is that which many felt, hearing Christ, when they were astonished at his doctrine. The next effect is the voice of thunder, which does not bring not only wonder, but fear also. Not only does it fill the ears with sound, and the heart with astonishment, but moreover shakes and terrifies the conscience. The third effect is the sound of harping, while the word not only ravishes with admiration, and strikes the conscience with terror; but also lastly, fills it with sweet peace and joy. Now, albeit, the two first degrees

> may be without the last, yet none feel the last, who have not in some degree felt both the first."

What is said here is true, in some degree, though commonly we must note that the deeper the sense of misery is, the sweeter is the sense of mercy.

Section 5: The Means to be delivered out of the Pangs of the New Birth.

1. And now if (by God's blessing), you feel this sorrow and melting of heart, the next thing you must do, is to seek for the remedy, which remedy consists of these ingredients. First, a sight of Christ. Secondly, a desire after Christ. Thirdly, a relying on Christ. Fourthly, an obedience to Christ. Fifthly, a comfort in Christ sought for and obtained. You will say, these ingredients are pearls indeed, but how should I obtain them? I answer, by application to the promises; and since every ingredient has its particular promises, I shall let you see them in order, only do apply them yourself. Some may object, I do not dare look to the promise, *I cannot believe*; if I could believe, then I could expect good from the promise. I answer, you shall never believe on these terms if you think that way. You must not first have faith, then go to the promise, and from there

receive power to believe. O! then go to the promise, and expect faith from there; this is the rule, "I must not bring faith to the promise, but to receive faith from it, and therefore there will I hang, and wait until the Lord is pleased to work it."

Section 6: The Promises Procuring a Sight of Christ.

The first step that brings comfort to your heavy soul is the sight of Christ: and to procure this sight you have these promises.

Matthew 1:2, "Thou shalt call his name Jesus, for fie shall save his people from their sins." John 1:29, "Behold the Lamb of God which taketh away the sins of the world." John 3:16, "God so loved the world, that he gave his only begotten Son, to the end that all that believe in him should not perish, but have life everlasting." Rom. 3:25, "God hath set forth Christ Jesus to be a reconciliation through faith in his blood." 1 Cor. 1:30, "Christ Jesus of God is made unto us wisdom, and righteousness, and sanctification, and redemption." 1 Tim. 1:15, "This is a true saying, and by all men worthy to be received, that Christ Jesus came into the world to save sinners." 1 John 2:1-2, "If any sin, we have an advocate with the Father, Jesus Christ the righteous, and he is the propitiation for our sins, and not for us only, but also for the sins of the whole world."

All these tell you, that as you are a sinner, so you have a Savior; only do apply them, and certainly they will help you in the first step of this remedy, in other words, the sight of Christ.

Section 7: The Promises Procuring a Desire after Christ.

You may say, I see Christ, and I see that his person, and death, and blood-shed are precious and saving; but how may I make him *mine*? How may I know that he is my Savior? I answer, you must hunger and thirst after him; this desire is the second step. And to provoke you to this duty, consider these promises.

Isa. 55:1, "Ho, every one that thirsteth, come ye to the waters, and he that hath no money, come ye, buy and eat; yea come, buy wine and milk without money, and without price." John 7:37-38, "In the last day, that great day of the feast, Jesus stood and cried, saying, if any man thirst, let him come unto me and drink; he that believeth on me, as the scripture hath said, out of his belly shall flow rivers of living water." Rev. 22:17. "Let him that is a thirst come, and whosoever will, let him take the water of life freely."

These may provoke you to thirst after Christ, that sovereign fountain, opened to the house of David, and to the inhabitants of Jerusalem for sin, and for uncleanness.

Section 8. The Promises Procuring a Relying on Christ.

Yet you may say, I thirst indeed, but I dare not drink; I desire, but I dare not come near, to lay hold on Christ. I am a most vile, unworthy wretch, and my sins are of a scarlet die: it is true, for you to pretend a part in Christ, wallowing yet in your sins; for you to believe that Christ is your righteousness, purposing to go on in any one known sin, is a most cursed, horrible presumption indeed. But all sin is a burden, and there a man may be bold. A man may? Yes, he *must*; if you groan under sin, if you long after Christ, apply these promises, and they will force you to lay hold on the rock, to take Christ for your own; to throw your sinful soul on the bleeding wounds of Jesus, and to cast yourself with confidence into the bosom of his love.

Matthew 12:28, "Come unto me all ye that labor and are heavy laden, and I will give you rest." Isa. 55:1, "Ho, every one that thirsteth, come ye to the waters, and he that hath no money; come ye, buy, and eat; yea, come, buy wine and milk without money and without price." And lest you say, I am so far from bringing anything in my hand, that I bring a world of wickedness in my heart, and my sins, I fear, will hinder my acceptation. But he says "no." Isa. 55:7, "Let the wicked forsake his way, and the unrighteous man his thoughts: and let him return unto the LORD, and he will have mercy upon him; and to our God, for he will abundantly pardon." If all this will not do without a more solemn invitation, see how the Lord of heaven sends forth his ambassadors to entreat you to come in. 2 Cor. 5:20, "Now then we are ambassadors for Christ, as though God did beseech you by us; we pray you in Christ's stead be ye reconciled unto God." Or if he cannot *woo* you, see, he *commands* you. 1 John 3:23, "And this is the commandment, that we should believe on the name of his Son Jesus Christ." Or yet to drive you to Christ, he not only commands, but threatens you. Heb. 3:18, "And to whom sware he that they should not enter into his rest, but to them that believed not?" How is it possible, but that all, or some of these, should bring in every broken heart to believe, and every one that is weary of his sins, to rely upon the Lord of life for everlasting welfare.

SECTION 9: THE PROMISES PROCURING OBEDIENCE TO CHRIST.

And yet you may say, I have cast myself on Christ, but is this all I must do? No, there is yet another step; he is not only to be your Savior, but your husband; you must love him, and serve him, and honor him, and obey him; you must endeavour not only for pardon of sin, and salvation from hell, but for purity, obedience, ability to do or suffer any thing for Christ. And to provoke you to this duty, consider these texts. Jer. 31:33, "But this shall be the covenant that I will make with the house of Israel; After those days, saith the LORD, I will put my law in their inward parts, and write it in their hearts; and will be their God, and they shall be my people." Matt. 7:21, "Not every one that saith unto me, Lord, Lord, shall enter into the kingdom of heaven; but he that doeth the will of my Father which is in heaven." Matt. 11:29. Take my yoke upon you, and learn ,of me, for I am meek and lowly in heart, and ye shall find rest unto your souls." Matt. 16:24. If any man will follow me, let him lake up his cross and follow me." 2 Cor. 5:15, "He died for all, that they which live, should not henceforth live unto themselves, but unto him which died for them." 1 John 1:6-7, "If we say we have fellowship with him, and walk in darkness, we lie and do not the truth. But if we walk in the light, as he is in the light, we have fellowship one with another: and the blood of Jesus Christ his Son cleanseth us from all sin." 1 John 2:5-6, "But whoso keepeth his word, in him verily is the love of God perfected: hereby know we that we are in him. 6 He that saith he abideth in him ought himself also so to walk, even as he walked." 1 John 3:6, 9, "Whosoever abideth in him sinneth not. Whosoever is born of God, doth not commit sin, for his seed remaineth in him, and he cannot sin because he is born of God."

All these may invite you to enter into the holy path, and to fight under Christ's banner against the world, the flesh, and the devil, to your life's end.

PART 3:
THE PRACTICE AND BEHAVIOR OF A MAN IN THE NEW BIRTH

The occasion of this part of the treatise.

Here, I have laid out the doctrine and application of the soul-saving *second birth.* There are some whose hearts are so hardened that all this cannot work on them. If any such desire yet any more (and desire they must, or there is no remedy for them), I have, for their help in the practice, brought a practitioner before them. It was Caesar's great praise that he told his soldiers *come.* And if men had but many Caesars or leaders in these practical points, I suppose there would be more followers. A plain doctrine may win some, and a particular direction may more, but a good example wins most. However then, concerning the *new birth*, I have delivered the doctrine in the *Sermons and Directions* in the appendix. Yet one thing is lacking, which may help more than either, in other words, the practice of some Christian in this one necessary thing. And what Christian? What man that has written more on this subject than T.H.? It was said of the blessed Mr. Robert Bolton, that for himself, he could profess to his comfort on his deathbed that he never taught any godly point, that did not believe in his own heart. The same could be said for his practice. Now therefore, I thought it fit to list in this appendix (which outsiders have unsuccessfully tried to do), and set before you the powerful expressions, the innermost thoughts about the New Birth, so you too can follow them. These innermost thoughts that I am aiming to express are told in first person. I truly believe they were not insincere, but came from his own heart and soul. If either *Doctrine* in the first part, or *Direction* in the second part, or *Practice* in the third part of the book (which consists mostly of *Practice)*, can work on your souls, I hope some or all of these, will help you on your way from corruption to Christianity; from the natural man to the spiritual Kingdom of Grace.

Isaac Ambrose

CHAPTER 1:
THE SOUL'S PREPARATION

Before the soul can share in Christ's merits (to use the author's words), two things are required:

1), A preparation to receive and entertain Christ.

2), An implantation of the soul into Christ.

That there must be a preparation, is the first point, and we *observe,*

The *matter.*

The *manner.*

And the *means*, of this preparation.

1. For the *matter*: the soul of a sinner must be prepared for Christ, before he can entertain Him. When kings go to any place, there are harbingers before them. If Christ, the King of Saints, comes into a soul, there must be a preparation before He enters. And this for good reason, he is not a mere man, nor an ordinary person, but a King, a *King of Glory*. David, in this case could call upon his soul, *Lift up your head, O ye gates, and be ye lifted up, ye everlasting doors, and the King of Glory shall come in.* Who should say, *be enlarged*, for *Love, joy, and hope are* set open, given away, for the Lord is coming, *But who is the Lord? It is the Lord of*

Hosts, the Lord strong and mighty the Lord mighty in battle. And with that He knocks again, *Lift up your heads, O ye gates, and be ye lifted up, ye everlasting doors, and the King of Glory shall come in,* as if he should say, What shall the Lord knock? Shall the King of Glory stand? Open it suddenly, and all get ready with preparation.

2. The manner of the preparation consists in these three passages: first, the soul breaks the condition which it formerly had in its corruption, and reserves itself for Christ. And secondly, the soul is most willing to give way to Christ Jesus and let him overthrow whatsoever shall oppose Him. Thirdly, the soul is content that God should rule everything, not only the eye, or hand, or tongue, but the whole man. It opens all the gates, and desires Christ to come, and take the keys to every room of the house to Himself.

3. The means of preparation is the powerful ministry which God has appointed for this work. And it is discovered in three parts. First, in a particular application of the truth to the souls of men with courage. Secondly, in a confirmation of the truth by soundness of argument, and plain evidence of the Scriptures. Thirdly, in a kind of spiritual heat in the heart and affections of the minister, which is reflected in the way he communicates to people. And this powerful ministry works on the soul in the following *manner:*

1), By discovering what is in a man's heart so that the soul sees what it never saw before, and so it is established.

2), By driving the soul into an awe of sin, so that it does not now meddle with sin, as it had in the past.

If any soul that has enjoyed these means for a while and is not so prepared, it is a fearful thing to consider that God will never confer any good on that soul. Go home then and reason with your soul, and plead in your own hearts, saying, *Lord, why am I not yet humbled and prepared? Will exhortations never prevail with me? Will terrors and reproofs never break my heart into pieces? I have heard sermons that would have shaken the very stones I trod on, that would have moved the very feet I stand on. The very fire of hell has flashed in my face. I have seen even the plagues of hell, and if anything can do me any good, why not those exhortations, admonitions, and reproofs that I have often had? I have witnessed powerful means, but none have yet been effective.* The Lord be merciful to such a poor soul, the Lord turn the heart of such a poor sinner, that He may lay hold of mercy in due time.

CHAPTER 2: GOD'S PART AND MAN'S PART

Section I. The General Circumstance of Preparation on God's Part.

But for further discussion, we shall consider two parts:

1), The general circumstances.

2), The substantial parts.

The general circumstances are twofold: God's part, and man's part.

God's part:

1), The offer of Christ and grace.

2. The condition of this offer.

3. The easiness of this condition.

Man's part:

1), Corruption opposes this grace.

2), God will remove this corruption.

The first general circumstance of the soul's preparation is on God's part, with the offer of Christ Jesus, the condition of this offer, and easiness of this condition. We may have all this in one comparison. As with a malefactor convicted of high treason, plotting some wicked thing against the Prince, if the King makes a proclamation that that person shall be pardoned but the person refuses. But if the King sends message after message to the person, that if he lay down his arms, he will be forgiven and restored to favor but the traitor would rather cast aside the pardon, will not the King raise an army and execute the traitor without mercy? I appeal to your conscience, is that not a just reward? What will the world say? He had a fair offer of pardon, and the King sent messenger after messenger to him, but he rejected all the offers. It is a pity, but he should be condemned. All would agree. This is the condition of every poor soul under heaven, we are all rebels and traitors, by our oaths and blasphemies we set our mouth against heaven. Yet, after all our pride and stubbornness, and looseness and profaneness, and contempt of God's Word and ordinances, the Lord is pleased to proclaim mercy still to everyone who will receive it. "All you that have dishonored my Name, All you that have profaned my Sabbaths, and condemned my ordinances, All you cursed wretches come, come who will, and take pardon." There is the offer. Only let them lay aside their weapons, that is the condition. Let them have Christ for the taking; there is the easiness of the condition.

"Blessed God (may every soul say), if I will not do this for Christ, I will do nothing. Had the Lord required a great matter of me to have attained salvation, had he required thousands of rams, and ten thousand rivers of oil, had He required the firstborn of my body for the sins of my soul, had he required me to have kneeled and prayed until my eyes had failed, until my hands had been wearied, until my tongue had been hoarse, and until my heart had fainted, one drop of mercy at the last gasp would have stopped the cost. But what goodness is this that the Lord should require nothing of me, but to lay down my weapons, and to receive Christ offered?" The Lord this day has sent from heaven, and offered salvation to the sons of men. The Lord Jesus is become a suitor to you, and I am Christ's spokesman, to speak a good word for Him. O, that we might have our way with you! O, "that there were such a heart in my people (*says the Lord*), to fear me, and keep my commandments always!" Shall the Lord and His messengers beg and plead in this way? And will any stand against God and say, "I want none of Christ, I will try it out later?" Then, if the great God of heaven and earth shall come with ten thousand judgments and execute them upon that man, if He shall bring a whole legion of devils, and say, "Take him, devils, and torment him, devils, in hell forever, because he would not have mercy when it was offered, he shall not have mercy, because he would not have salvation when it was offered, let him be condemned." If God should in this way deal with that man, the Lord should be just in so doing, and that man be justly miserable.

Section 2: The general circumstance of the soul's preparation, is on man's part, and is *observable:*

1), That corruption opposes grace.
2), That God will remove corruption.

The first is clear. 1 Cor. 2:14, "The natural man receiveth not the things of the Spirit of God, neither can he know them," and Acts 7:51, "Ye stiff necked and uncircumcised in heart and ears, ye do always resist the Holy Spirit, as your fathers did, do ye." Give us a man in the state of nature, and though all ministers under heaven should preach mercy to him, though all the angels of heaven should exhort and entreat him, though all glory and happiness were laid before him, and he were wished only to believe it in order to take it forever, in his natural condition he has no power to receive so blessed an offer. However, this does not hinder, but only causes him to wait on God.

Secondly, God may remove this corruption, which man cannot do. Here, we observe the author and time of this grace.

First, the author is *God.* "I will take away their stony hearts (*God says*), and give them a heart of flesh." I will remove that sturdy heart which is in them, and will give them a framable, teachable heart, which shall be pliable and yield to whatever I teach them. The taking away of the indisposition of the soul and fitting, framing and disposing it to perform spiritual service: that is the work of God alone.

Quiet then your soul, and content your heart; you might say, "I have an hard heart within, and it will receive no good from without, the Word will not prevail, the sacraments do not have power over me, all the means God has bestowed on me are lost, and my heart is not yet humbled, my corruptions are not yet weakened." But be comforted in this, though the means cannot do it, which God uses at His pleasure, yet the Lord can do it. There is nothing too difficult for Him.

Be exhorted, you who have stony hearts, to have recourse to this great God of heaven. Should a physician set up a cure for every disease, and we all heard about it, this might stir people up to go to him. But the Lord has set up a place to cure all of their stony hearts if they will only come to Him, and all the children of God know it, to the comfort of their souls. You wives that have husbands with stony hearts, you parents that have children with stony hearts; tell them you have a heart this day of a physician that will cure them, and exhort them to come to Him.

Secondly, the time of this grace is either in regards of:

1), The means.

2), The men.

1. In regard of the means, and that is, when sons of men have the gospel, the gospel shining in their faces, if ever there was a good work in their hearts, it will be then.

This should teach us how thankful we ought to be to the Lord, that enjoy these liberties in the land of the living. That he was born at such a time, in the last days of the world, in this place, in this Kingdom, where the way of life and salvation is so fully, plainly and powerfully made known that the sun of the gospel shines fully in his face, and has not yet set. O how thankful he should be!

And for those that neglect the means of their salvation, how should we pity them? I think I see a poor creature that slighted mercy and salvation when it was offered him. I think I see that soul lying upon his death bed, light departing from his eyes, and his soul is departing from his body. O the name of a minister of a church, they are as bills of indictment against the soul of this man. I think I hear such a man say at his last gasp, "The day is gone, the gate is shut, and now it is too late to enter." And thus the soul departs from his body to the grave, and to hell. O what bitter lamentation will that soul make in hell, "O the golden time that I have seen, and not regarded! O the gracious opportunities of salvation that my eyes have beheld, and yet I neglected! O the mercy and grace, and goodness of God, that have been offered to me! All these I have condemned, and trampled under my feet, and therefore now I must be tormented with the devil and his angels, from everlasting to everlasting." Now the Lord gives us hearts to take notice of these things. If I were now breathing out my last breath, I would breathe out this legacy to all surviving Christians, "This is the accepted time, this is the day of salvation." Do you hear? This day is grace offered, and if any here would entertain it. O, what comfort might he have. "I was never humbled, he might say, but this day I was humbled, I could never before receive mercy, but this day I received it. O this was a good day to me, how blessed am I forever."

2. In regards to men on whom God works, that is to say, on some in their tender age. But however the Lord does at several times convert several of his servants, yet most are before their old age, and that some interpreters wittily observe out of the Parable of the Vineyard, Matt. 20:3-5, "The master of the vineyard (the text says), went out at the third, sixth and ninth hour, and saw some standing idle, and he sent them into his vineyard." He went then (interpreters say), on purpose to see and hire, and to send in laborers to work in his vineyard, but he went out at the eleventh hour not to hire any, he did not expect then to see any who were idle. He went out upon some other occasion and when he saw them standing, he wondered and said, "Why are you here idle all day?" As if to

say no man will hire you now, because it is almost nighttime. It is not a time to leave work or to begin working.

O, let this provoke us while the flower is in its prime, that we ought to use all means for our good, let us now in the heat and summer of our days, improve ourselves in good works, so that when Christ comes we are not ashamed as his servants.

CHAPTER 3: GOD'S WORK ON THE SOUL

The substantial parts of preparation on God's part, or his dispensations of his work on the soul is considered next.

Here are the general circumstances of the soul's preparing for Christ. Now the substantial parts of this preparation are *generally:*

1), The dispensation of God's work on the soul.

2), The dispensation of the soul by God's work.

The dispensation of God's work discovers itself in drawing the soul:

1), from sin.

2), to himself.

But because these two are made up by one action and motion, we shall therefore handle them together, and the sum is this, that "God by an holy kind of violence (which is called *drawing*, John 6:44), plucks the soul from those sins that harbor in it to himself. In which we may consider two *things:*

1), What the nature of this drawing is.

2), The means whereby God draws.

First, for the nature of this drawing, it is of a double *kind:*

1. There is a moral drawing, when by reasons propounded, and good things offered to the understanding and will, a man comes to have his mind enlightened, and his will move to embrace things offered. So it was with Paul, when he was constrained by Lydia to abide in her house, Acts 16:15. 2. There is a physical drawing, when the Lord is pleased to put a new power into the soul of a sinner, and with it to carry the will to the object propounded, that it may embrace it, when the Lord not only offers good things to the soul, but enables the soul to lay hold upon the things offered. And in this way the Lord draws a sinner from sin to himself.

Secondly, for the means by which he draws, they are these four.

First, the Lord lets in a light into the soul of a poor sinner, and reveals to him he is in a wrong way. This the soul marvels at, because usually it comes on suddenly, the sinner perceives it. (*cf.* Isaiah 56:1).

Secondly, though a man would defeat the power of this light, yet God still follows it with forcible arguments, and draws with the cord of his mercy. "I taught Ephraim to go (God says), taking them by the arms. I drew them by the cords of love, and with the bonds of a man." This mercy consists of these bonds, or this love is made up of four cords.

1. The Lord reveals Himself to be ready to receive, and willing and easy to entertain poor sinners when they come to Him. "Let the wicked (the Prophet says), forsake his way, and the unrighteous man his thoughts, and let him return unto the Lord, and he will have mercy upon him, and to our God, for he will abundantly pardon." The word in the original is, "He will multiply pardons." The bowels of compassion are still open, and the arms of mercy are still spread abroad. He pardoned Manassas, and Paul, and Peter, and so will he you also. His pardons are multiplied, because there is yet mercy for you also, and for a thousand more.

2. The Lord is not only ready to forgive when men come to Him, but only ready to forgive *that they may come.* He also calls *and* commands them. "O but may I (a poor sinner says), shall I, dare I go unto the Lord God for mercy? May I be so bold to press in for favor at the hands of the Lord? I have been a grievous sinner, and have heaped abomination upon abomination, I am afraid therefore to approach near unto the Lord's preference." Is it so? Hear what the Lord says, "Come unto me, ye rebellious people, and I will heal your rebellions. You that never prayed, never came to hear, all rebels, come to me." And then people answer, "Behold, we come unto thee, for you are our God." This is great encouragement to a poor sinner, he begins now to wonder, and say, "Lord shall all my sins be pardoned? Shall all my oaths and abominations be

forgiven? I that slighted so many mercies, and committed so many follies, shall I be entertained? Yes (the Lord says), come to me, and you shalt be forgiven, come, I command you come."

3. The Lord does not only command a poor sinner to come in, but when he is nice in this case, saying, "There is mercy with God, but not for me." The Lord then follows him still, and sends another cord after him, that if it is possible he may win him, and woo him to receive mercy of him. If commands therefore do not prevail, he entreats and beseeches him to come and receive mercy, and this (I think), should move the hardest heart under heaven. "We (the Apostle says), are ambassadors for Christ, as though God did beseech you by us, we pray you in Christ's stead, be reconciled unto God," rather then you should go away from Christ, even mercy itself will come and kneel down before you, and beseech you, and entreat you, "for it is the Lord Jesus' sake to pity your poor souls, and to receive pardon for your sins." A sinner is not able to comprehend this, but he begins to be at a stand, and at amazement, "What that the Lord should beseech him! O that you would receive pardon for your sins, and be blessed forever! Good Lord (the soul says), is this possible, that the great king of heaven should come and seek out such a traitor, such a rebel as I am, to take pardon? That a king on earth should proclaim a pardon to some notorious traitor, this were much, but that the King of Heaven should lay down his

crown, and come creeping to me, and seek me (on his knee as it were), to take mercy, this is a thing beyond all expectation. What, shall heaven stoop to earth? Shall majesty stoop to misery? Shall the great God of heaven and earth, that might have condemned my soul, and if I had perished and been damned, might have taken glory by my destruction. Is it possible, is it credible, that his God should not only entertain me when I come, and command me to come, but entreat and seek me to come and receive mercy from him? O the depth of the incomprehensible love of God!" Imagine that you saw God the Father entreating you, and God the Son beseeching you, as he does this day, "Come now, and forsake your sins, and take mercy, which is prepared for you, and shall be bestowed upon you." Would not this make a soul think thus with itself, "What for a rebel? Not only to have mercy offered, but to be entreated to receive mercy, it were pity (if I will not take it), but I should go to hell and be damned forever." The Lord complains, "Why will ye die?" As I live, saith the Lord, I desire not the death of a sinner. Turn ye, turn ye, why will ye die, ye sinful sons of men? Mercy is offered you, the Lord Jesus reacheth out His hand to you." He desires to pluck the drunkard out of the alehouse, and the adulterer from his whore. O! if you break this cord, I do not know what to say to you, this is able to break a mountain in pieces. "Shake, Oh mountains," (the Prophet says). Why? "Because God hath redeemed Jacob." The redemption of Jacob was enough to break a mountain, let his mercy break our hearts, it is God that begs, the blessing is our own.

4. If yet all this prevails nothing at all, the Lord will then wait, and stay in long patience and suffering, then see if any time a sinner will turn to Him. Our Savior follows poor sinners from alehouse to alehouse, and says, "I beseech you, drunkards, take mercy, and have your sins pardoned." The Lord (as we may say), tires himself, wearies himself with waiting one day after another, and one week after another. "It may be (Christ says), this week, this Sabbath, this sermon a sinner will turn unto me, what, will it never be?" Are you not ashamed (my friends), that the Lord Jesus should thus wait your leisure, and follow you from house to house, and from place to place, no that Christ should every morning appear to your understanding and every night come to your bedside saying, "Let this be the last night of sinning, and the next day the first day of your repentance. O when will you be humbled? When will you receive mercy, that it may go well with you, and with yours forever?" If none of the other will move you, yet for shame let his cord draw you to the Lord. Hear, hear His doleful pangs, "O Jerusalem, Jerusalem, wilt thou not be made clean? O when will it once be?" A woman that is in travail, O how she expects and longs for her delivery! Now a throb comes, and then she cries, and then a second throb, and the

cries again, "O when comes deliverance?" Thus God the Father takes on Him the person of a travailing woman, He travails and travails until He brings forth a Son, until some soul be converted, and brought home unto Him, "O Jerusalem, wilt thou not be made clean? When will it once be? I have waited one, ten, twenty, thirty, forty years long have I waited on this generation, when will it once be?" The Lord in this way travails in patience, looking toward the time they will receive mercy. Will our proud hearts ever be humbled? Will never our stubborn hearts be softened? Will never our profane hearts be sanctified? When will it once be? Christ has waited this day, this week, this month, this quarter, this year, these ten, twenty, thirty, forty years on us. You old sinners, that are grey-headed in your wickedness, how long has the Lord waited on you? O for shame let him wait no longer, but turn, turn unto him, that you may receive mercy from him.

Thirdly, if bonds of love do not move you, the Lord has iron cords that will pluck to pieces the cords of conscience. "He that is often reproved, if he still hardens his heart, shall perish everlastingly."

In this syllogism are monition, accusation, and condemnation of conscience.

In the first proposition, conscience gives the sinner a monition, to come from sin, on pain of the heaviest judgment that can be inflicted. It is the Lord that sends the conscience on this errand, "Go to such a man, and tell him, you have blasphemed God's Name, and you have spoken against God's saints, and you have broken God's Sabbaths, and you have condemned God's ordinances. Be it known then to you (conscience says when it delivers the message), that I have a command from heaven, and from God, I charge you, as you will answer it at the dreadful day of judgment, take heed of those evils and sinful practices that before you have committed, lest you damn your souls forever." Will you question His commission? See Proverbs 29:1, "He that being often reproved hardeneth his neck, shall suddenly be destroyed." If you are often reproved, and will not be bettered, then the Lord says, and conscience from the Lord tells you, "Be it at your own peril, you shall suddenly be destroyed." No sooner is conscience pricked than the sinner withdraws himself from his former lewd courses. But now when wicked persons see their companion is gone, they sway back, and at last, with carnal company and cursed persuasions, the soul is drawn back again to his former wicked course. And so, perhaps the cord is broken and the sinner is gone.

2. If so, then conscience, that was a monitor, now turns to be an *accuser* in the minor proposition. Before it was only God's herald to forewarn him, but now it is become a sergeant to arrest him. It follows him to the alehouse, and pursues him home, then takes him to bed, and arrests him in

his sleep, there (by a meditation), it hails the soul before the tribunal feat of God, saying, "Lo, Lord, this the man, this is the drunkard, adulterer, blasphemer, this is he, Lord, and enemy to your servants, a hater of your truth, one who defies your ordinances. At such a time, in such a place, with such a company this man defied your truth, this is he, Lord, this is the man. And when conscience has in this way dragged him before God, and accused him, then "Take him Devil (the Lord says), and imprison him, let vexation, and horror, and trouble, and anguish lie upon his soul, until he confess his sins, and resolve to forsake them." In this case was David, when he was forced to say, "My bones waxed old through my roaring all the day long, for day night your hand was heavy upon me, my moisture is turned into the drought of summer." What then? "O then (David says), I acknowledged my sin unto thee, I confessed my transgressions unto thee, O Lord, and so thou forgave the iniquity of my sin." David folded up his sins at first, and therefore his bones were consumed, and he roared continually, when the Lord had him on the torture table, he made him roar again, and would never leave tormenting, until David came to confessing, but when he confessed this sin, and the other sin, then the Lord forgave him the iniquity of his sin. In this way conscience brings the soul of a sinner on the rack (as traitors are used, that will not confess otherwise), and makes him to confess his sins, and then cries, "O the abominations I have committed which the Son never saw, in such a place, at such a time, O then I railed on God's servants, and blasphemed God's Name, I profaned God's Sabbaths, and condemned his ordinances," what then? Conscience will make him confess more yet, to the rack again with him, and then he cries and roars for anguish of spirit, then he confesses all, and resolves to amend, then he will pray, and hear, and sanctify God's Sabbaths, and lead a new life. This is way conscience receives some satisfaction and begins to be quiet, and now having got some quiet, his cursed companions set upon him again, refresh (they say), your soul with some of your ancient dalliance, and the rest. To this and the same type of the temptations of Satan, he listens again, and then he begins to follow his old sins, perhaps with more violence and eagerness than ever he did before, and now another tie is also broken.

3. If so, then conscience that was a monitor and accuser now turns to executioner. The first proposition admonished, the second accused, if neither of these prevail, then conscience concludes, "You must execute, you shall perish everlastingly." And now conscience cries, "Monitions or accusations could not prevail with this man. Come, come you damned ghosts, and take away this drunkard, this blasphemer, this adulterer, and throw him headlong into the pit of hell, he would not change, let him be condemned, he would not be humbled, therefore let him be damned." The

man hearing this, then he is amazed, and thinks himself past hope, past help and past cure. Did you ever see or hear a tormented conscience in these pangs? Now he calls and then he cries, "Lo where devils stand, the heaven's frown, God is incensed, hell's mouth is open." And now a minister is sent for, who displays to this despairing soul, the mercy and grace of God in Christ Jesus, "O, (he replies), this is my bane, my damnation, if I had never heard of mercy, if I had never lived under the gospel, and the means of salvation, then had I been a happy man. Alas! It is mercy I have neglected, it is salvation I have condemned, how then should I be saved? O, the persuasions of the Lord that I have had! The Lord has even wept over me, as he did over Jerusalem. O that you would have known the things belonging to your peace! Yet all these persuasions have I condemned, and therefore certainly to hell I must go." The minister replies, the truth is, you have done this, but will you *still* do it? Is it good now to be drunk, or to blaspheme, or to rail at God's saints, or condemn God's ordinances? "O no, no (he says), I now find what the end of those wicked courses will be. God's Word could not prevail with me, the minister could not persuade me, O the good sermons that I have heard, the very flames of hell have even flashed in my face, the Minister has spent his time, and would have spent his blood for the good of my poor soul! But alas, I despised the Word, and mocked the minister. Woe, to me forever, now my conscience gnaws, and tears, and terrifies my soul here, and I shall go to hell hereafter, and perish for ever and ever. The minister replies again, the truth is, you have done this, but would you do so *now*? Would you *still* blaspheme, and curse and be drunk, and riotous? Or rather, would you not now part with all these and take mercy instead of them? Then the poor soul cries out, "Now the Lord for his mercies sake remove these sins from me. O I had never so much delight in my sins heretofore, as now I have so much woe and vexation for them. But (alas), it is not in my power to help my soul. If the Lord would do this, let him do what he will with it." What (the Minister says), you are then willing and content to part with your sins. "O yes, (the soul says), I would rather offend the entire world than God. I had rather go to hell, then to commit a sin. If it would please God to help me, I would forsake my sins with all my heart." Why now the poor soul is coming again, and God is drawing him again from his corruptions and sinful distempers.

Fourthly, when the soul is in this way loosened, the Lord then fully plucks it by the cord of His Spirit. With an Almighty hand he cuts the soul off from sin, and takes it into his own hand, that he may govern him, and dispose of Him according to his own good will and pleasure. This much of preparation of substance is on God's part.

CHAPTER 4: THE DISPOSITION OF THE SOUL

Section 1: Let us consider the substantial parts of the preparation on man's part, or the disposition of the soul by God's work.

Now are we to observe the disposition of the soul on man's part, which God works on the hearts of whom He draws. It is known in two *works:*

1), contrition, by which the soul is cut off from sin.

2), humiliation, by which the soul is cut off from itself.

For so it is, that either the soul sees no need to depart from sin, or else it thinks it can help itself out of sin. The first is called *security*, when the soul being blind, takes rest, and seeing no need to be better, does not desire it. Against this the Lord sends contrition, causing men by it to know the misery of sin, and to see need of a change. The second is carnal confidence, when a sinner begins to seek, succor, and to scramble for his own comfort in his self-sufficiency. Against this the Lord works humiliation, causing the soul by it to see the weakness and emptiness of its duties, and that there is enough in its best services to condemn him forever. Before we speak of the works, it is not improper to begin with the means.

The first is security. When the soul rests on itself and is satisfied with its own practices, and therefore does not see any need to change. Now, while a man lives this way, and is content in his sin, it is impossible that he should ever receive faith, or by the power of faith receive Christ. Where faith comes, it works change, "Old things are done away, and then all things become new." The Lord therefore removes the hold and burdens the soul greatly, and says, "You will live in drunkenness, in covetousness, you will have your sins, then take your sins, and get down to hell with them." At this voice the sinner begins to see where he is. "Is this true? (he says), then I am the most miserable creature under heaven," therefore as they said, "Men and brethren, what shall we do? We have been this way and that way, but if we rest here, it will be our ruin forever, O what shall we do?" So the soul comes to a restless dislike of itself, and says, "I must either be otherwise, or else I am a damned man forever."

2. When the soul is in this way resolved that it must of necessity change, when it sees his wound and his sin ready before him to condemn him, and it has (as it were), a little peep-hole into hell. The soul in this distress sends over to

prayer, and hearing and holy services, and thinks by his wits and duties, or some such matters, to succor itself, and it begins to say, "My hearing and my prayer, will not these save me?" So the soul in conclusion rests on duties. I will not say but these duties are all good, honorable and comfortable, yet they are not God's but the *ordinances* of God. It is the nature of a sinful heart, to make the means, as meritorious as salvation. A man that sees his drunkenness and base contempt of God, O then he vows and promises to take a new course, and he begins to approve himself in reformation of his ways, then he cries, "Now I will have no more drunkenness, now no more scoffing and scorning at those that go to hear the Word." And then he thinks, "What can I do more? To heaven I must go." All this is but a man's *self*. Why so? Christ (who is the substance of all), and the substance of the promise is forgotten. Christ hearing and praying is disregarded and therefore the poor soul dies of hunger. Do not misunderstand, I pray, these duties must be had and used, but still a man must not stay here. Prayer says, "There is no salvation in me," and the sacraments and fasting say, "There is no salvation in us," yet all these are subservient helps, not the *cause* of salvation. A man will use his bucket, but he expects water to come from the well. The means is the bucket, but all our comfort, and all our life and grace is only in Christ. If you say, your bucket shall help you, you may starve for Christ, if you do not let it down into the well for water. So, though you boasts of praying, and hearing and fasting, and of your alms, and building hospitals, and of your good deeds, if none of these bring you to Christ, or settle you on Christ, you shall die without Christ, even though your works were like those of an angel. As it is with a graft, first it must be cut off from the old stock. Secondly, it must be pared, and made fit for implantation into another. So the soul, by contrition being cut off from sin, then humiliation pares it (pares away all a man's privileges), and makes it fit for the engrafting into Christ Jesus.

So much of the means, of the works of contrition and humiliation in general.

Section 2: A Sight of Sin. But for a further discovery of these two necessary things, we shall now enter into particulars, and begin first with contrition, which contains these *steps:*

1. A sight of sin.
2. Sense of divine wrath.
3. Sorrow for sin.

The first step is a sight of sin, clearly, convincingly.

First, clearly. It is not a general sight, and confused sight of sin that will suffice. It is not enough to say, "It is my infirmity, and I cannot change it, we are all sinners." No, this is the grounds on which we mistake our evils, and do not change our ways. A man must search narrowly, and prove his ways, as the goldsmith does his gold in the fire. "I considered my ways, (David says), and turned my feet unto thy testimonies, in the original, I turned my sins upside down," he looked over all his ways. And this clear sight of sin appears in two *ways:*

1. A man sees his sin nakedly in its own true colors. We must not look on sin through the mediums of profits and pleasures, and contentments of this world, for if we do, we mistake sin. But the soul of a true Christian that would see sin clearly, he must strip it of all content and quietness that ever the heart receives in it. As the adulterer must not look upon sin in a sweet way, nor the covetous man on his sin in a longing way, you that are such must die and then consider what these sinful ways will do to you. How will you judge the sin then, when it shall leave a blot on your souls, and a guilt on your consciences?

2. A man must look on sin in its venom, and that you may do partly, if you compare it with other things, and partly, if you look at it in relation to itself.

1. Compare sin with those things that are most fearful and horrible, as suppose any soul here present were to behold the damned in hell, if the Lord should give any one of you a little peep-hole into hell, that you saw the horror of the damned, then take this to heart, what are those pains which

the damned endure, and your heart will shake and quake at it. Yet the least sin that you ever committed is a greater evil in its own nature than the greatest pains of the damned in hell.

2. Look at sin simply as it is in itself, what is it but opposing God Himself? A sinful creature joins on the side of the devil, and comes in battle array against the Lord, and flies in the face of the Lord God of Hosts. I pray that you in cold blood consider this, and say, "Good Lord, what a sinful wretch am I? That a poor damned wretch of the earth, should stand in defiance against God! That I should submit myself to the Devil, and oppose the Lord of Hosts!"

Secondly, sin, in and of itself, may be so obvious it reveals itself in *two ways:*

1. When we have a particular understanding in our self, that whatever sin is in general, we confess the same in our soul. It is the cursed distemper of our hearts, however much we hold to the truth in general, that when it comes to our own sin, we deny it. The adulterer confesses the filthiness of that sin in the general, but will not apply it to himself. The rule there is, "Arrest your soul (whosoever you are), of those sins particularly of which you stand guilty." To this purpose, say, is murder and pride, and drunkenness and uncleanness such horrible sin? O Lord, it was my heart that was proud, and vain, it was my tongue that did speak with filth and blasphemy. It was my hand that brought wickedness, my eye

that was wanton, and my heart that was unclean and filthy. Lord, here they are. So bring your heart before God.

2. When the soul sits down with the audience of truth, and seeks to not oppose truth revealed, when the Lord comes to change a heart that He means to do good, the text says, "He will reprove the world of sin," that is, "He will convince the world of wickedness." He will set the soul in such a way that it shall have nothing to say for itself, and he has nothing to say about it. The minister says, God hates such and such a sinner, and the Lord hates me too (the soul says), for I am guilty of that sin. So many times, when a sinner comes into the congregation (if the Lord is pleased to work on him), the mind is enlightened, and the minister meets with his corruptions, as if he were in his bosom, and he answers all his cavils, and takes away all his objections. With that the soul begins to have faith, "If this is so (as it is for all I know), and if all is true that the minister says, then the Lord be merciful to my soul, I am the most miserable sinner that ever was born."

You that do not know your sin, that you may see them convictingly, get you back to the Law, looking at that, and bundling up all your sins so that, "Many sins against God himself in the *First Commandment*, against his worship in the second, against his Name in the third, against his Sabbath in the fourth. In all our thoughts, words and actions, all of them have sins in them, such that they would sink our souls to the bottom of hell."

And secondly, that you may see them clearly, consider their effect, both in their doom and in their execution. I think I see the Lord of heaven and earth, and the attributes of God appearing before him; the mercy of God, the goodness of God, and the wisdom of God, the power of God, the patience and long-suffering of God, and they all come to a sinner, a hypocrite, or to a carnal professor, and say, mercy has relieved you, goodness has succored you, wisdom has instructed you, power has defended you. Patience has born with you, longsuffering has endured you, now all these comfortable attributes will bid you farewell, a damned soul, you must go to hell, to have your fellowship with the damned ghosts. Mercy shall never more relieve you, goodness shall never more succor you, wisdom shall no more instruct you, power shall never more defend you, patience shall never more bear with you, longsuffering shall never more endure you. And then you go to endless torments without end, where you will always remember your sin, and say, my covetousness and pride was the cause of this, I may thank my sins for this. Think of these things (I beseech you), seriously, and see your sins here, to prevent this fight in the hereafter.

Section 3: Sense of Divine Wrath. The sinner, by this time having his eyes so far opened, that he beholds his sins, he begins to consider, that God has him in chase. And this sense of divine wrath discovers itself in these *two ways:*

1), It works a fear of evil to come.

2), It possesses the soul with a feeling of this evil.

First, the soul considers, that the punishment which God has threatened shall be executed on him sooner or later. He cries therefore, "What if God should damn me? God may do it. And what if God should execute his vengeance on me?" So the soul fears, that the evil discovered will fall on him. This is the reason of those phrases of Scripture, "We have not received the bondage to fear again," the Spirit shows our bondage, and from that comes this fear. Again, "God hath not given us the spirit of fear," that is, the spirit of bondage that works fear. It is with a soul in this fear, as it was with Belshazzar, when he commanded the cups to be brought out of the house of the Lord, "An handwriting came against him on the wall, and when he saw it, his thoughts troubled him, and his face began to gather paleness, and his knees knocked against one another," as if he should have said, "Surely there is some strange evil appointed for me," and with that his heart began to tremble and shake. Just so it is with this fear; he runs riotous in the way of wickedness, and thinks to despise God's spirit, and to resist the work of His grace. Now it may be that there comes "this fear and handwriting against him," and then he cries, "These are my sins, and these are the plagues and judgments threatened against them, and therefore why may not I be damned? Why may not I be plagued?"

Secondly, the Lord pursues the soul, and discharges that evil on him which was formerly feared, and now his conscience is all on a flame, and he says to himself, "O I have sinned, and offended a just God, and therefore I must be damned, and to hell I must go." Now the soul shakes, and is driven beyond itself, and would utterly faint, but that the Lord upholds it with one hand, as he beats it down with the other, he thinks, everything is against him, he thinks the fire burns to consume him, and that the air will poison him, and that hell gapes under him, and that God's wrath hangs over him, and if now the Lord should but take away his life, that he should tumble down headlong into the bottomless pit of hell. Should any man, or minister, persuade the soul in this case to go to heaven for mercy, it replies in this manner, "Shall I return to God?" O, that is my trouble! Is not He that great God, whose justice, and mercy, and patience I have abused? And is not He the great God of heaven and earth that has been incensed against me? O, with what a face can I appear before him, and with what heart can I look for any mercy from him? I have wronged his justice, and can his justice pardon me? I have abused his mercy, and can his mercy pity me? What, such a wretch as I am? If I had never enjoyed the means of mercy, I might have had some plea for myself, but O, I have refused that mercy, and have trampled the blood of Christ under my feet, and can I look for any mercy? No, no I see the wrath of the Lord incensed against me, and that is all I look for.

Section 4: Sorrow for Sin. The next step is sorrow for sin, concerning which are *two questions:*

1. Whether it is a work of saving grace?
2. Whether God works it in all alike?

To the first, I answer, there is a double sorrow, one in preparation, the other in sanctification. They differ in this way, sorrow in preparation, is when the Word of God leaves an impression on the heart of a man, so that the heart of itself is as it were a patient, and only bears the blow of the Spirit, and here comes all those phrases in Scripture, such as "wounded, pierced, pricked," in the passive voice, so that this sorrow is rather a sorrow worked on me, then any work coming from any Scriptural ability in me. But sorrow in sanctification flows from a spiritual principle of grace, and from that power which the heart has formerly received from God's Spirit, so that in this a man is a free worker. Now, both of these are saving sorrows, but they differ marvelously, many think, that every saving work, is a sanctifying work, which is false, "Those whom he calleth (the Apostle says), them he also justifies, and whom he justifies, he glorifies." You may observe, that glorification in this place implies sanctification here, and glory hereafter, now glorification, you see there is justification and vocation, and both of these are saving.

To the second answer, however, this work is the same in all for substance, yet in a different manner it is worked in most. Two men are pricked, the one with a pin, the other with a spear, two men are cut, the one with a pen knife, the other with a sword. So the Lord deals kindly and gently with one soul, and roughly with another. There is the melting of a thing, and the breaking of it with hammers. So there is a difference in persons. For instance, if the person is a scandalous liar, he opposes God and His grace. Secondly, if a man has harbored a filthy heart, and continues long in sin. Thirdly, if a man has been confident in a formal civil behavior. Fourthly, if God purposes by some man to do some extraordinary great work. In all these four cases he lays a heavy blow on the heart, the Lord will bruise that person, and wrench the heart and make them seek a faithful minister for direction, and a poor Christian who they previously despised for counsel. But if the soul is trained up by godly parents, and lives under a soul saving ministry, the Lord may reform this man, and cut him off from his corruptions completely, and break his heart secretly, in the understanding of the depth of his sin, and yet the world never sees it. In both of these we have an example in Lydia and the jailer. Lydia was a sinful woman, and God opened her eyes, and melted her heart kindly, and brought her to taste of His goodness here, and glory hereafter. But the jailer was an outrageous, rebellious wretch, for when the Apostles were committed to prison, he laid them up in stocks, and whipped them sorely; so there was now much work to bring this man home. When the Apostles were singing Psalms there came an earthquake, which made the prison doors fly open, and the prisoner's fetters to fall off, but yet the jailer's heart would not shake. At last *the Lord* shook his heart too, and he came trembling, and was ready to lay violent hands on himself, because he thought the prisoners had fled, but the Apostles cried to him, "Do yourself no harm, for we are all here." With that, he fell down before the apostles, and said, "Men and brethren, what must I do to be saved?" In conclusion, give me a Christian that God is pleased to work on in this extraordinary manner, and to break his heart profoundly, and to throw him down for a purpose, though it cost him much, this man walks ordinarily with more care and conscience, and has more comfort coming to himself, and gives more glory to God.

Is it so, that the soul of a man is thus pierced to the quick, and run through by wrath of the Almighty? Then let this teach all how to carry themselves towards such as God has dealt with us. Are they pierced men? O, pity them! Let our souls, O let the bowels of commiseration and compassion be let out towards them! Let us never cease to do good to them, to the very uttermost of our powers! And to the performance of this, reason and religion, and pity (I think), should move us. Hear the cry, O (says the poor soul), will these sins never be pardoned? Will this proud heart never be humbled? So the soul sighs and mourns, and says, O Lord, I see this sin, and feel the burden of it, and yet I have not a heart to be humbled for it, nor to be freed from it. O when will it once be? Did you but know this, it would make your hearts bleed to hear him. O! The sword of the Almighty has pierced through his heart, and he is breathing out his sorrow as though he were going down to hell, and he says, If there is any mercy, any love, any fellowship of the Spirit, have mercy on me a poor creature, that I am, under the burden of the Almighty! O, pray, and pity these wounds and vexations of spirit, which no man finds nor feels, but he that has been wounded. It is a sign of a soul wholly devoted to destruction, that has a desperate disdain against poor, wounded creatures. Is it possible that there should harbor such a Spirit in any man? If the devil himself was incarnate, I cannot conceive what he would do worse.

2. If you would ever be comforted, and receive mercy from God, labor never to be quiet, until you bring your heart to a right pitch of sorrow, you have a little slight sorrow. O! Labor to have your heart truly touched, that at last it may break in regard to your much unsettledness, remember, the

long seed time, the greater the harvest. "Blessed are they that mourn, for they shall be comforted, but woe to you, that are at ease in Zion." Though they had better now be wounded, then everlastingly tormented, and therefore if you desire to see God's face with comfort, if you would hear Christ say, "Come thou poor heavy hearted sinner, I will ease thee," labor to lay a load on your heart, with sorrow for your sin. O, what a comfort shall a poor broken heart find in that day!

Section 5: The extent of this sorrow. Until this time we have discussed contrition. The next work is humiliation, which differs from the others, not in substance, but in circumstance. For humiliation is only the extent of sorrow for sin, which we have spoken about, and it contains these two *duties:*

1), submission, and,

2), contentedness, to be at the Lord's disposal.

The first part of humiliation is submission which is brought about in this way: the sinner having had sight of his sin, and sorrow in some measure for them, seeks far and wide, improves in every way possible and tries in every way possible to heal his wounded soul. This seeking, and seeking after, but finding no relief in what he has or does, is forced at last (in his despairing condition), to make an appeal to the Lord. It is true, for the present he understands God to be just, and to be incensed against him, he has no experience of God's favor for a while, no certainty of how he shall do if he goes to the Lord, yet because he sees he cannot be worse than he is, and that none can help him but God, if it would please Him. Therefore, he falls at the footstool of mercy, and lies groveling at the gate of grace, and submits himself to the Lord, to do with him as He pleases and as it seems good in His eyes.

This was the Ninevites case when Jonah had denounced the heavy judgment and threw wildfire about the streets saying, "Within forty days Ninevah shall be destroyed." See what they resolved upon, "They fasted, and prayed, and put on sackcloth and ashes, who can tell (they said), but God may turn and repent Him of His fierce wrath, that we do not perish? As if they had said, we do not know what God will do, but this we know, that we cannot oppose His judgments, nor relieve ourselves. So it is with the sinner, when he sees hell fire to flash in his face, and that he cannot relieve himself, then he says, this I know, that all the means in the world cannot save me, yet who can tell, but the Lord may have mercy on me, and cure his troubled conscience, and heal all these wounds that sin has made in my soul? This is the lively picture of the soul in this case.

Or for a further light, this subjection discovers itself in *four ways:*

First, he sees and confesses that the Lord (for he knows), will proceed in justice against him, and execute upon him those plagues take God has threatened, and his sins have deserved, he sees that justice is not yet satisfied, and those reckonings between he and God are not yet made up, and therefore he cannot understand, but that God will take vengeance on him. What else? When he has done all that, he is unprofitable still. Justice remains unsatisfied, and says, you have sinned, and I am wronged, and therefore you shall die.

Secondly, he conceives that what God will do, that he will do, and he cannot avoid it, if the Lord will come, and require the glory of his justice against him, there is no way to avoid it, nor to bear it. And this crushes his heart, and makes the soul to be beyond all avoidances and evasions, where it seems to avoid the destruction of the Lord's blow.

Thirdly, he puts away his weapons, and falls down before the Lord and resigns himself to the sovereign power and command of God. In this way, David, when the Lord cast him out of his kingdom, he said to Zadok, "Carry back the ark of God into the city, if I shall find favor in the eyes of the Lord, He will bring me back again, and shew me both it and His habitation. But if he thus says to me, I have no delight in thee, behold here I am, let him do with me as seemeth good in His eyes." This is the frame of a poor soul, when a poor sinner will stand upon his privileges, the Lord says, bear my justice, and defend yourself by all you have or cannot do. And the soul answers, I am your servant, Lord, do what is good in your eyes, I cannot relieve myself.

Fourthly, the soul freely acknowledges that it is in God's power to do with him, and dispose of him as He will, and therefore he lies and licks the dust, and cries, mercy, mercy Lord. He does not think to purchase mercy at the Lord's hands, but only faith, it is in God's good pleasure to do with him as he will, only he looks for favor, and cries, Mercy, Lord, mercy to this poor distressed soul of mine. O, (the Lord replies), do you need mercy? Cannot your hearing, and praying and fasting carry you to heaven without danger of hell? Gird up your loins and make your most fervent prayers, and let them meet my justice, and see if they can bear my wrath, or purchase any mercy. No (the sinner says), I know it by lamentable experience, that all my prayers and performances will never procure peace to my soul, nor give satisfaction to your justice, I only pray for mercy, and I desire only to hear some news of mercy to relieve this miserable wretched soul of mine. It is only mercy that must help me. O, mercy (if it is possible), to this poor distressed soul of mine. I think the picture of those poor famished lepers, may fitly resemble this poor sinner, when the famine was great in Samaria. "There were four leprous men seated in the gate of the city, and they said, why sit here until we die? If we enter into the city, the famine is there, and if we sit here, we die also. Now therefore let us fall into the hands of our enemies, and if they favor us alive, we shall live, and if they kill us, we shall but die." They had but one means to relieve themselves, and that was to go into the camp of the enemy, and there, as it happened, they were relieved. Thus is the lively picture of a poor sinner in this despairing condition, when he sees the wrath of God pursuing him, and that the Lord has beset him on every side. At last he resolves within himself, if I go and rest on my privileges, there is nothing but emptiness, and if I rest in my natural condition, I perish there also. Let me therefore fall into the hands of the Lord of Hosts. I confess, He has been provoked by me and as far as I can tell is my enemy. I am now a damned man, and if the Lord cast me out of his presence, I can be but damned. And then he comes to the Lord, and he falls down before the footstool of a consuming God, and says, as Job did, "What shall I say unto thee, O thou preserver of men? I have no reason to plead for myself, and I have no power to relieve myself, my accusations are my best excuse, all the privileges in the world cannot justify me, and all my duties cannot save me, if there is any mercy left, O relieve a poor distressed sinner in the very gall of bitterness. This is the behavior of the soul in this work of subjection.

The second part of humiliation is contentedness to be at the Lord's disposal, and this point is of a higher pitch than the former. For example, take a debtor who has used all means to avoid the creditor, in the end he sees he cannot avoid a lawsuit, and to bear it he is not able, therefore the only way is to come in, and to yield himself into his creditors hands. But suppose the creditor should exact the utmost, and throw him into prison, to be content now to undergo the hardest dealing, it is a hard thing, an extreme thing. So when the soul has offered himself, and he sees that God's warrants are out against him, and he is not able (whenever the judgment comes), to avoid it, not to bear it, therefore he submits himself, and says, Lord where shall I go? Your anger is heavy and unavoidable, and whatever God requires, the soul lays his hand on his mouth, and goes away contented, and well satisfied, and has nothing at all to say against the Lord. This is the nature of contentedness.

Or for a further point, this contentedness discovers itself in these *three ways:*

First, the soul reflects on God's mercy, which though he begged when he submitted, yet now he sees so much corruption and unworthiness in himself, that he acknowledges himself unfit for mercy. O, mercy Lord! What (the Lord says), I had thought your own duties would have purchased mercy. O no (the soul says), it is only mercy that must relieve and comfort me, but such is my vileness that I am not fit for the least mercy and favor, and such is the wickedness of this wretched heart of mine, that whatsoever are the greatest plagues, I am worthy of them all, though never not insupportable. All the judgments that God has threatened, and prepared for the devil and his angels, they are all due to my wretched soul. O (the soul says), had the devils had the time, ability and forbearance I have enjoyed, for what I know, they would have been better than I. It is that which shames the soul in all his sorrows, and makes him say, Had they the same mercy? O those sweet comforts, and those precious promises that I have had! How many heavy journeys has the Lord Jesus made to me? How often has he knocked at my heart, and said, "Come to me, ye rebellious children, turn ye, turn ye, why will ye die?" O that mercy that has followed me from me around room to room, and to my closet, here mercy has conferred with me, and there mercy has wooed me. Yes, in my night thoughts when I awakened, mercy kneeled down before me, and besought me to renounce my bad ways, yet I refused mercy and would have my own will, had the devil but such hopes, and such offers of mercy, they that tremble now for want of mercy, they would (for all I know), have given thought to it, and how can I now seek mercy? Shall I talk of mercy? What, mercy for me? The least of God's mercies are too good for me, and the heaviest of God's plagues are too little for me. I suppose (it is my opinion), that God cannot do more against me than I have justly deserved, but be sure, God will not lay more upon me than I am justly worthy of. No, sure as it is, the soul cannot bear nor suffer so much as he deserves, if God should deal with him in all rigor. Therefore, the soul reasons like *this:* "I only for one sin deserve external condemnation, for the wages of all sin is death, being committed against divine justice and against an infinite majesty. And then, what do all my sins deserve, committed deliberately and continued, against all conscience and correction, and the light of God's Word? Hell is too good, and ten thousand hells too little torment for such a wretch as I am. What? Do I expect mercy? I am ashamed to even expect it. With what heart may I beg this mercy, which I have trodden under my feet? The Lord has often wooed me, and when His wounds were bleeding, and his side gored, and hideous cries came into my ears, *My God, My God, why have you forsaken me?* Then, even then this Christ I have slighted, and made nothing of His blood, can this blood now do me service? Indeed I crave grace, but how can I even dare to receive any? All the pillars of the church can testify, how often grace and mercy have been offered, time and time again, but I have refused. How then can I beg for any grace? O, this stubbornness and villainy, and this wretchedness of mine! What, mercy? It is more than I can expect, I am not worthy of any of it. O no, I am only worthy of being cut off forever."

Secondly, the soul reflects on justice, and now it acknowledges the equity of God's dealing, be they never so harsh. He confesses that he is as clay in the hands of the Potter, and the Lord may deal with him as he wills. Yes, the soul is driven to an amazement at the Lord's patience, and that he has been pleased to give him a reprieve for so long. That God has not cast him out of his presence, and sent him to hell long ago. It is the frame of the Spirit which the poor lamenting church had. It is the Lord's mercy that we are not confounded, because his compassions fail not. When the Lord has humbled the heart of a drunkard or adulterer, He begins to think to himself, The Lord saw all the evils I committed, and what will happen? O, then the soul admires that God's justice was able to bear such a monster, and that God did not confound him in his drunkenness or burning incense and cast him down to hell. O (he says), it is because His mercies fail not, that my life and all have not failed long ago. Here it is that the soul will not maintain any kind of murmuring, or heart rising against the Lord's dealings. Or, if nature and corruption will be striving sometimes, and say, why are not my prayers answered? I know such a soul humbled and I see such a soul comforted and why not I as well as he? Then the soul strikes, and crushes and chokes these wretched distempers, and abases itself before the Lord saying, what if God will not hear my prayers? What if God will not pacify my conscience, does the Lord do me any wrong? Vile hell-bound that I am, I have my sin and my shame. Wrath is my portion, and hell is my place, and there I will go, but it is mercy that God has and deals that way with me. And now the soul clears God in His justice, and faith, It is just with God that all the prayers which come from this filthy heart of mine, should be abhorred, and that all my labors in holy duties should never be blessed. It is I that have turned against checks of conscience, against knowledge, against heaven, and therefore it is just that I should carry this horror of heart with me to the grave. It is that I have abused mercy, and therefore it is just that I should go with a tormenting conscience down into hell. And O that (if I am in hell), I might have a spirit to glorify and justify your Name there, and say, now I am come down to hell among you damned creatures, but the Lord is righteous and blessed forever in all His doings and dealing, and I am justly condemned.

Thirdly, then the soul comes to be quiet and frames itself under the heavy hand of God in that helpless condition that it is in. It takes the blow, and lies under the burden and goes away quietly and patiently. O this is a heart worth gold! O (he says), is fit that God should glorify Himself though I am damned forever, for I deserve the worst. Whatsoever I have, it is the reward of my own works, and the end of my own ways. If I am damned, I may thank my pride, my stubbornness, and my possessiveness of spirit. What shall I repine against the Lord because His wrath and His displeasure lies heavy on me?

O no! Let me repine against my sin, the cause of all. Let me grudge against my base heart that has manifest these snakes in my bosom, but let me bless the Lord, and not speak one Word against Him. So, David, I hold my tongue (he says), and speak nothing, because the Lord has done it. So the soul, when the sentence of condemnation is even seizing upon him, and God seems to cast him out of his favor, then he cries, I confess, God is just and therefore I bless his Name, and yield to Him, but sin is the worker of all this misery on me. Jeremiah pleaded the case of the church, now going to captivity, "Woe is me for my hurt (he says), my wound is grievous, but I said, truly this is my grief, and I must bear it." Such is the frame of a heart truly humbled, it is content to take all to itself, and so to be quiet saying, this is my wound, and I must bear it, this is my sorrow, and I will suffer it. So you see what is the behavior of the soul in this contentedness to be at the Lord's disposal.

Objection. But some may object, Must the soul, or ought the soul to be in this way content to be left in this damnable condition?

Answer. For answer, this contentedness implies two things: First, a carnal security, and a regardlessness of a man's estate, and this is a most cursed sin. Secondly, a calmness of soul, not murmuring against the Lord's disposition towards him, and this contentedness is ever accompanied with the sight of a man's sin, and suing for mercy. It ever improves all means and helps that may bring him nearer to God, but if mercy shall deny it, the soul is satisfied, and rests well paid. And this contentedness (as opposed to quarrelling with the Almighty), every humbled soul desires, although in every one it is not plainly seen. To give it by way of comparison: a thief caught in a robbery, on whom the sentence of death has been passed, should not neglect the means to get a pardon. And yet, it he cannot procure it, he must not murmur against the judge for condemning him to death, because he had done nothing but what the law requires. So we should not be careless in using all means for our good, but seek God for His mercy. Yet this we must be, and so we must be content with whatever mercy shall deny, because we are not worthy of *any* favor. The soul in a depth of humiliation, first stoops to the condition that the Lord will appoint, he dares not fly away from God, nor repine against the Lord, but he lies down meekly. As he is content with the hardest measure, so he is content with the longest time, he will stay for mercy no matter if it is never so long. "I will wait upon the Lord (*Isaiah says*), that hath hid his face from Jacob; and I will look for him." So the humbled sinner, although the Lord hide His face, and turn away his loving countenance from me, yet I will look towards heaven, so long as I have an eye to see, and a hand to lift up, the Lord may take his own time, it is appropriate for me to wait. No, the poor broken heart resolves, that if I lie sick and in the dust all my days and cry for mercy all my life long, if my last words might be mercy, mercy, it were well that I might get mercy at my last gasp. Thirdly, as he is content to stay the longest time, so is he content with the least pittance of mercy. Let my condition be never so hard (the soul says), do Lord what you will for me, let the fire of your wrath consume me here, only restore me in the life to come. If I find mercy at the last, I am content, and whatever you give, I bless your Name for it. He does not quarrel saying, why are not my graces increased, and why am I not comforted? No, he looks for mercy, and if he has but a crumb of mercy he is comforted and quieted forever. And now (you may suppose), the heart is brought very low.

Therefore we *understand*,

1. That they which have the greatest parts and gifts and ability and honor are (for the most part), hardly brought home to the Lord Jesus Christ. They that are most hardly humbled are most hardly converted. What is humiliation, but the emptying of the world from whatever makes it well. The heart must not joy in anything, nor rest upon anything, but only yield to the Lord, to be at his disposing and carving. Now these parts, and gifts, and abilities, and means are great props and pillars for the heart of a carnal man to rest upon, and to quiet himself with. When the Apostle said, "Not many wise men after the flesh, not many mighty men, not many noble

men are called," indeed (blessed be God), some are, but not many, few (that have so much of themselves), are brought to renounce themselves, and no wonder for a rich man to become poor, and a noble man to be abased, and a wise man to be nothing in himself, this will cost hot water. And yet this must be in all that belong to the Lord. Not that God will take away all these outward things and parts, but that they must loosen their affection from these, if they will have Christ.

2. That a humble heart makes all a man's life quiet and marvelously sweetens whatever estate he is in. Indeed, sometimes he may be tossed and troubled, yet he is not distracted because he is contented, as it is with a ship on the sea, when the billows begin to roar, and the waves are violent. If the anchor is fastened deep, it stays the ship. So this work of humiliation is the anchor of the soul, and the deeper it is fastened, the more quiet is the heart. When Job in time of his extremity gave way to a proud heart, he quarreled with the Almighty, his friends, and everyone. But when the Lord had humbled him, then "Behold, I am vile, and base, and once have I spoken, yea twice, but now no more."

And this humiliation quiets a man *both in:*

1), fiercest temptations.

2), heaviest oppositions.

1. In fiercest temptations, when Satan begins to besiege the heart of a poor sinner, and lays battery against

him, see how the humbled heart runs him out of breath at his own weapons. Do you think (Satan says), to get mercy from the Lord, when your own conscience dogs you? No, go to the place where you live and to the chamber where you lie, and consider your fearful abominations, surely God will not respect the prayers of any such vile sinners. True (the poor soul says), I have often denied the Lord when he called upon me, and therefore he may justly deny me all the prayers I make, yet thus he has commanded, that I must seek him for mercy, and if the Lord will cast me away, and reject my prayers, I am contented there to say, what then, Satan? What then, says the devil? I thought his would have made you to despair, but this not everything, for God will give you over and leave you to yourself, to your lusts and corruptions, and your latter end shall be worse than your beginning. You may call and cry and when you have been overthrown, God will leave you to yourself, and suffer your corruptions to prevail against you, and you shall fall fearfully, to the wounding of your conscience, to the grieving of God's people, to the scandal of the gospel, to the reproach of your own person. To this answers the humbled soul, If the Lord will give me up to my base lusts, which I have given myself to much liberty in, and if the Lord will leave me to my sins, because I have left His gracious commands, and if I shall fall one day, and be disgraced and dishonored, yet let the Lord be honored, and do not let God lose the praise of His power and justice, and I am contented therewith- what then, Satan? What then says the devil? I surely thought now that you would have despaired, but this is not the whole story. When God has left you to your sins, then he will break out in vengeance against you, and make you an example of his heavy vengeance for all ages to come. And therefore it is best for you to prevent this untimely judgment by some untimely death. To this replies the soul, Whatsoever God can do or will do, I do not know, yet so great are my sins, that he cannot, or (at least), will not do so much against me as I have justly deserved. Come what will come, I am contented still to be at the Lord's disposal, what then Satan? And, in this way, he runs Satan out of breath.

The lack of this humiliation many times brings a man to a desperate place, and sometimes to an untimely death. Alas, why will you not bear the wrath of the Lord? It is true indeed, your sins are great, and the wrath of God is heavy, yet God will do you good by it, and therefore, be quiet. In time of war, when the canons fire, the only way to avoid them is to lie down in a furrow so the bullets fly over. So, in all temptations of Satan, lie low, and be contented to be at God's disposing, and all these temptations shall not be able to hurt you.

2. In heaviest oppositions. When Satan is gone, then comes troubles and oppositions of the world, in all of which, humiliation will quiet the soul. A man is sometimes seasick,

not because of the tempest, but because of his full stomach, and therefore when he has emptied his stomach, he is well again. So it is with his humiliation of heart, if the heart were truly emptied, though a man were in a sea of opposition, if he have no more trouble in his stomach, and in his proud heart, then in the oppositions of the world, he might very well be quieted. Cast disgrace on the humble heart without care, and he cures it this way. He thinks worse of himself than any other man does, and if they would regard him as vile and loathesome, he is more vile in his own eyes then they can make him. O, that I could bring your hearts to be in love with this blessed grace of God!

Is there any soul here that has been vexed with temptations of Satan, oppositions of men, or with his own distempers? And would he now arm and protect himself, that nothing should disquiet him, or trouble him, but in all, to be above all, and to rejoice in all? O then be humbled, and then be above all the devils in hell. Certainly they shall not disquiet you, as to cause you to be miffed, or uncomforted, if you would be but humbled.

What remains then? Be exhorted (as you desire mercy and favor at God's hands), to this humiliation. And for motives, consider the good things that God has promised, and which he will bestow on all that are truly humbled. I shall reduce all of this to three benefits:

First, by humiliation we are made capable of all those treasures of wisdom, grace and mercy that are in Christ.

Secondly, humiliation gives a man the comfort of all that good in Christ. Many have a right to Christ, and are dear to God, yet they want much sweet refreshing, because they want this humiliation in some measure. To be truly humbled is the next way to be truly comforted. The Lord will look to him that has a humble, contrite heart, and trembles at His Word. The Lord will not only know him (he knows the wicked too in a general manner), but He will give him such a gracious look, as shall make his heart dance in his breast. You poor humbled soul, the Lord will give you a glimpse of His favor, when you are tired in your trouble, when you look up to heaven, the Lord will look down upon you, and will refresh you with mercy. God has prepared a sweet morsel for His child, He will revive the humble. O be humbled then, every one of you, and the Lord Jesus, who comes with healing under His wings, will comfort you, and you shall see the salvation of our God.

Thirdly, humiliation ushers glory. "Whosoever humbles himself as a little child, shall be greatest in the Kingdom of heaven." He shall be in the highest degree of grace here, and in glory thereafter. For as your humiliation goes, so shall be your faith, and sanctification, and obedience, and glory.

And now, I think, your heart begins to stir, and say, Has the Lord engaged Himself to do this? O then, Lord, make me humble. Now the Lord makes me, and you, and all of us humble, that we may have this mercy. See how everlasting happiness and blessedness looks and waits for every humbled soul. Come, faith, happiness, you that have been vile, and base and mean in your own eyes, come and be greatest in the Kingdom of heaven. Brethren, though I cannot prevail with your hearts, yet let happiness, that kneels down, and prays you to take mercy, let that, I say, prevail with you. If any man be so regardless of his own good, I have something to say to him that may make his heart shake within him. But O! Who would not have the Lord Jesus to dwell with him? Who would not have the Lord Christ, by the glory of His grace, to honor and refresh him? I think your heart should yearn for it, and say, O Lord, break my heart, and humble me, that mercy may be my portion forever, no, I think every man should say as St. Paul did, "I would to God that not only I, but all my children and servants were not only thus as I am, but also (if it were God's will), much more humbled, that they might be much more comforted and refreshed." Then might you say with comfort on your death bed, though I go away and leave wife and children behind me, poor and mean in the world, yet I leave Christ with them. When you are gone, this will be better for them, than all the beaten gold or honors in the world. What can I say? But since the Lord offers so kindly, now kiss the Son, be humble, yield to all God's commands, take home all truths, and be at God's disposing. Let all the evil that is threatened and all the good that is offered prevail in your hearts, or if it cannot, let the Lord prevail with you and empty you, that Christ may fill you. The Lord humble you, that you may enjoy happiness and peace, and be lifted up to the highest pinnacle of glory, there to reign for ever and ever.

CHAPTER 5:
GOD'S CALL

Next we will consider the Call on God's part, for the soul to close with, and to rely on Christ.

Up to now, our first general proposition has been the preparation of the soul for Christ. The next is, the implantation of the soul into Christ, and that has *two parts:*

1. The putting of the soul into Christ.
2. The growing of the soul with Christ.

As a graft is first put into the stock, it then grows together with the stock. These two things are answerable in the soul, and when it is brought into this, then a sinner comes to be a partaker of all spiritual benefits.

The first part is, the putting in of the soul. When the soul is brought out of the world of sin, to lie upon, and to close with the Lord Jesus Christ, and this has two particular passages. We shall *look at,*

The call on God's part.

The answer on man's part.

The call on God's part is this, when the Lord, by the call of his gospel, and work of his Spirit, clearly reveals the fullness of mercy, that the soul humbled returns an answer.

In which observe the means, cause, by which God calls.

1. The means is *only* the ministry of the Gospel. The sum of it is this, that there is fullness of mercy, and grace, and salvation brought to us through the Lord Jesus Christ. Here, the phrase of Scripture calls this *gospel*, or this mercy, a treasury. All the treasures of wisdom and holiness are in Christ. Not one treasure, but all treasures. Where the gospel comes, there is joy for the sorrowful, peace for the troubled, strength for the weak, relief seasonable and suitable to all desires, miseries, and necessities, both present and future.

If then sorrow assails you when you have come this far, look not on your sins, to pour on them, neither look into your own sufficiency, to procure any good there. If it is true, you must see your sins, and sorrow for them, but this is for the lower form, and you must get this lesson beforehand, and when you have gotten this lesson of contrition and humiliation, look then only to God's mercy, and the riches of His grace *in Christ*.

2. For the cause. The Lord does not only appoint the means, but by the work of the Spirit, he brings all the riches of His grace into the soul truly humbled. How? First, with strength of evidence, the Spirit presents to the broken hearted sinner, the right of the freeness of God's grace to the soul. And secondly, the Spirit forcibly soaks in that grace, and by an

over-piercing work, leaves some residue of supernatural and spiritual virtue on the heart.

Now, the work of the gospel, and the work of the Spirit always go together, not that God is tied to any means, but that he ties Himself to the means. Here, the gospel is called the power of God to salvation, because the power of God ordinarily, and in ordinary course appears this way. The waters of life and salvation run only in the channel of the gospel, there are gold mines of grace, but they are only to be found in the climates of the gospel. No, observe this, when all arguments do not prevail with corruption, to persuade the heart to go to God, one text of Scripture will stand a man instead above all human learning and inventions, because the Spirit goes forth in this and in nothing else.

This may teach us the worth of the gospel above all other things in the world, for it is accompanied with the Spirit, and brings salvation with it. What if a man had all the wealth and policy in the world, and wanted this? He would be a fool. What if one were able to dive deep into the secrets of nature, to know the motions of the stars, to speak with the tongues of men and angels, and yet know nothing belonging to His peace, what avails it? Why do we value a mine, because of the gold in it? Or a cabinet, because of the pearl in it? O, this is that pearl we would sell everything for.

Do you know whether you are carnal or spiritual? Observe then, if you have the Spirit, it always came with the gospel. See how the soul stands affected with the gospel, and so it stands effected by the Spirit. Is it so (may every soul reason with itself), that I will not suffer the Word to prevail with me? Then shall I miss of the Spirit, then will Christ have none of me. O, remember, the time will come when you must die as well as your neighbors, and then you will, Lord Jesus forgive my sins. Lord Jesus receive my soul. But Christ will answer, away, be gone, you are none of mine, I do not know you. Any man, whether noble or ignoble, let him be what he will be, if he does not have the Spirit he is not of Christ. You are His to whom you obey. But pride and covetousness you obey. Pride therefore will say, this heart is mine, Lord, I have domineered over it, and I will torment it. Corruptions will say, we have owned this soul, and we will damn it. You therefore, that have made a jeer at the word, this wind shakes no corn, and these words break no bones, little do you think that you have opposed the Spirit. What, resist the Spirit? I think it is enough to sink any soul under heaven. Hereafter, therefore, think this within yourself, Were he but a man that speaks, yet would I not despise him. But that is not all, there goes God's Spirit with the Word, and shall I despise it? There is but one step between this and that unpardonable sin against the Holy Spirit, only adding malice to my rage. I oppose the Father, perhaps the Son mediates for me. I despise the Son, perhaps the Holy Spirit pleads for me, but if I oppose the Spirit, none can rescue me.

CHAPTER 6: CLOSE WITH CHRIST

Section 1: We must answer on Man's part for the soul to close with, and to rely on Christ.

After looking at the call on God's part, now we are come to the answer on man's part. No sooner has the gospel and God's Spirit clearly revealed the fullness of God's mercy in Christ, but then the whole soul (both the mind that discovers mercy, and hope that expects it, and desire that pursues it, and love that entertains it, and the will that rests on it), gives answer to the call of God in it. Mercy is a proper object of all these, of the mind enlightened, of hope to be sustained, of desire to be supported, of love to be cheered. No, there is a full satisfactory sufficiency of all good in Christ, so that the will of man may take full repose and rest in Him. Therefore the Lord says, "Come unto me, all that are weary and heavy laden," come mind, and hope, and desire, and love, and will, and heart. They all answer, we will come. The mind says, Let me know this mercy above all, and desire to know nothing but Christ and Him crucified. Let me expect this mercy (says hope), that belongs to me, and will befall me. Desire faith, Let me long after it. O, says love, let me embrace and welcome it. O, says the heart, let me lay hold on the handle of salvation, where we will live, and where we will die at the footstool of God's mercy. Thus all go, mind, hope, desire, love, joy, the will, and all lay hold upon the promise, and say, Let us make the promise our prey, let us prey upon mercy, as the wild beasts do upon their provision. Thus the faculties of the soul hunt and pursue this mercy, and lay hold thereupon, and satisfy themselves therein.

Section 2: The next section is a sight of Christ, or of mercy in Christ.

For a further discovery of these works of the soul, we shall now enter into particulars. And for their order, first, the Lord lets a light into the mind, for what the eye never sees, the heart never desires, hope never expects, the soul never embraces. If the soul then seems to stand far off, and does not dare believe that Christ will have mercy on him, in this case the Spirit lets a light into his heart, and discovers that God will deal graciously with him. It is with a sinner, as with a man that sits in darkness, and is in the dungeon all the while, and he thinks, how good were it, if a man might enjoy that light? So, many a poor humble hearted broken sinner sees, and has an inkling of God's mercies, he hears the saints speak of God's love, and His goodness, and compassion. Ah, he thinks, how happy are they, blessed are they, what excellent condition are they in? But I am in darkness still, and never had a drop of mercy explained to me. At last, the Lord sets a light in his house, and puts the candle into his own hand, and makes him see by particular evidence, you shall be pardoned, and you shall be saved.

The manner how the Spirit works this, is discovered in three passages.

First, the Spirit of the Lord meeting with a humble, broken, lowly, self-denying sinner (he that is proud, stout hearted is a wretch who knows nothing of this), opens the eyes, and now the humbled sinner begins to see, like the man in the gospel, some light and glimmering about his understanding, that he can look into, and discern the spiritual things of God.

2. Then the Lord lays before him all the riches of the treasure of his grace, no sooner has he given him an eye, but that he lays colors before him (the unsearchable riches of Christ), that he may see and look, and fall in love with those sweet treasures, and then the soul says, O that mercy, and grace, and pardon were mine! O that my sins were done away! The Lord says, I will refresh them that are heavy laden, then the soul says, O that I had that refreshing! You shall have rest, says God, O that I had rest too, the soul says! And now the soul begins to look after the mercy and compassion which is laid before it.

3. The Spirit of the Lord witnesses or certifies thoroughly and effectually to the soul, that this mercy in Christ belongs to him, and without this, the soul of a humble broken-hearted sinner has no basis on which to go to Christ. What good it does for a hungry stomach to hear that there is a great deal of cheer and dainties provided for such and such men, and he has no part in that? Take a beggar that has a thousand pounds put before him (he may understand the worth of such an amount of gold and silver), but what is all that to me, he says if in the mean time I die and starve? It falls out in this case with a broken hearted sinner, as with a prodigal child. The prodigal has spent his substance, and abused his father, and now there is famine in the land, and poverty has befallen him, he knows indeed there is meat and clothes enough in his father's house, but (alas), what can he expect there but his father's heavy displeasure? If a man should say, go to your father, he will give you a portion again, would he believe this? No, he would say, it is my father I have offended, and will he now receive me? Yet should a man come and tell him, that he heard his father say so, and then show him a certificate under his father's hand that it was so, this would sure draw him into some hope that his father meant well toward him. So it is with a sinner when he apprehends his rebellions. If a man should tell such a soul, go to God, and he will give you abundance of mercy and compassion, the soul

cannot believe it, but thinks, *What, mercy for me*? No, no. Blessed are they that walk humbly before God, and conform their lives to his word, let them take it, but for me, it is mercy I have opposed, it is grace I have rejected, no mercy, no grace for me. But now, if God send a messenger from heaven, or if it comes under the hand of his spirit that he will accept of him, and pass by all his sins, this makes the soul grow into some hopes, and upon this ground it goes to the Lord. But here observe me, that none either in heaven or in earth, but only God's Spirit can make this certificate, when it is night, all the candles in the world cannot take away the darkness, so all the means of grace and salvation, all the candle light of the ministry, they are all good helps, but the darkness of the night will not be gone, before the sun of righteousness arises in their hearts. Here it is, that it proves so difficult a matter to comfort a distressed soul, I shall one day perish, says David, I shall one day go down to hell. The soul says, let all the ministers under heaven cry, *comfort ye, comfort ye*. Still he replies, mercy for me? Comfort for me? Will the Lord pardon me? It is mercy I have despised and trampled under my feet, and I mercy? No, no. So we ministers observe by experience, some that in their own apprehensions are gone to the bottom of hell, we make known to them reasons, and arguments, and promises, but nothing takes place, what is reason? O none but God's Spirit can do it, he must either come from Heaven, and say comfort ye, comfort ye my people, or it will never prevail. Let me speak therefore to you that are ministers, you do well to labor to give comfort to a poor fainting soul, but always say, comfort Lord, O Lord, say unto this poor soul, that you are His salvation.

Section 3: We turn now to hope in Christ.

The mind being in this way enlightened, the Lord calls on the affections, come desire, come love. But the first voice is to hope. Now hope is a faculty of the soul that looks out for mercy, and waits for the same, so the Apostle says in Phil. 1:20. "According to my earnest expectation and my hope, that in nothing I shall be ashamed, but that with all boldness, as always, so now also Christ shall be magnified in my body, whether it be by life, or by death." The phrase, "according to my earnest expectation," is a similitude taken from a man that looks after another, and lifts up as high as he may to see if any is coming after him. So here the soul stands as it were a tip toe, expecting when the Lord comes, he has heard the Lord say, mercy is coming towards you, mercy is provided for you. Now this affection is set out to meet mercy afar off, it is the looking out of the soul. O when will it be Lord? You say mercy is prepared, you say mercy is approaching, the soul stands on tip toes, O when will it come Lord! Here is the voice of hope. This sinful soul of mine, it may through God's mercy be sanctified. This troubled perplexed soul of mine, it may through God's mercy be pacified, this evil and corruption which harbors in me, and has taken possession of me, it may through God's mercy be removed, and when will it be, Lord?

The manner in which God's Spirit works this is explained in *three ways:*

1. The Lord sweetly stays the heart, and fully persuades the soul, that a man's sins are pardonable, and that all his sins be pardoned, and that all the good things he lacked, those he may receive; this is a great sustainer of the soul. When a poor sinner sees his sins in their number, nature, when he does not see rest in the creature, nor in himself, though all means, all help, all men, all angels, should join together, yet they cannot pardon one sin of his, then the Lord lifts up His voice and says from heaven, your *sins are pardonable in the Lord Jesus Christ.*

2. The Lord sweetly persuades the soul that all his sins shall be pardoned, the Lord makes this appear, and persuades his heart that he intends mercy, that Christ has procured pardon for the soul of a broken-hearted sinner in special, and that he cannot but come to it, by this means hope comes to be assured, and certainly persuaded to look out, knowing the promise shall at last be accomplished. The former only sustained the heart, and provoked it to look for mercy, but this comforts the soul, that undoubtedly it shall have mercy. "The Lord Jesus came to seek and to save that which was lost." Now says the broken and humble sinner, I am lost. Did Christ come to save sinners? Christ must fail in his purpose or

I must fail myself in comfort. God says, "Come unto me, all you that are weary and heavy laden." I am weary, and unless the Lord intends good unto me, why should he invite me and bid me come? Surely he means to show me mercy, He promises to relieve me, when I come, therefore He will do good to me.

3. the Lord lets in some relish and taste of the sweetness of His love, some scent and favor of it, so that the soul is deeply affected with it, and carried mightily into it, that it cannot be severed. It is the including in on the riches of His love, that turns the expectation of the soul another way, yes, indeed, it turns the whole course of the soul in that direction.

This reproves, 1), those that cast off hope, and 2), those that without grounds will do nothing but hope. 1), If the Lord stirs up the heart of his to hope for his mercy, then take heed of that fearful sin of despair. We must despair in ourselves, and that is good, but this despair we speak of, is heinous in the eyes of God, and hurtful for you.

1. Injurious to God, you go to the deep dungeon of your corruption, and there you say, these sins can never be pardoned, I am still proud, and more stubborn, this distress God does not see, God rescues not, his hands cannot reach, his mercy cannot save. Now make a note what the Prophet says to such a perplexed soul, "Why do you say that your way is

hidden from the Lord?" The Lord says, Why do you say that? Is anything too hard for the Lord? O you wrong God exceedingly; you think it a matter of humility, when you give such a vile account of yourself. Can God pardon sin to such unworthy creatures? It is true (the soul says), Manasseh was pardoned, Paul was converted, God's saints have been received into mercy, but can *my* sin be pardoned? Can my soul be quickened? No, no, my sins are greater than can be forgiven. Why then, poor soul, Satan is stronger to overthrow you, then God to save you. So, you make God to be no God. You make Him to be weaker than sin, than hell, than the devil.

2. This sin is dangerous to your own soul. It is that which takes up the bridge, and cuts off all passages, it even plucks up a man's endeavors (as it were), quite by the roots. Alas, he says, what point is there to pray? What profit it a man to read? What benefit is there in the means of grace? The stone is rolled on me, and my condemnation sealed forever. I will never look after Christ, grace, salvation any more. The time of grace is past, the day is gone. And so the soul sinks into itself, Will the Lord cast me off forever, and will he show no favor? "I said (David says), this is my infirmity." The word in the original is, "This is my *sickness*," as who should say, what is mercy gone forever? This will be my death, then life is gone.

2. This reproves and condemns that great sin of presumption, a sin more frequent, and (if possible), more

dangerous, as they said, *Saul had slain his thousands, and David his ten thousands.* So has despair slain his thousands, but presumption his ten thousands. It is the counsel of Peter, that every man should be ready to give an account of this faith and hope that is in him. Let us see the reasons that persuade you to these groundless foolish hopes? You say, you hope to be saved, and you hope to go to heaven, and you hope to see God's face with comfort, and have you no grounds? It is a foolish hope, and unreasonable hope.

But comfort yourself, poor drooping spirits. "They that wait upon the Lord shall renew their strength." You say, You cannot do this, and you cannot do that. I say, if you can but hope, and wait for the mercy of the Lord, you are rich Christians. If a man has many reversions, they that judge of his estate, will not judge him for his present estate, but for the reversions he shall have. Happily you do not have for the present the sense and feeling of God's love and assurance, with that feeling, and you do not dote on it; you have reversions to old leases, ancient mercies, old compassions, such as have been reserved from the beginning of the world, and know you have a fair inheritance.

You will say, were my hopes of the right stamp, then I might comfort myself, but there are many false, flashy hopes, and how should I know that my hope is sound and good? I answer, you may know it by these *particulars:*

1. A grounded hope has a peculiar certainty in it, it does bring home to the soul in a special manner, the goodness of God, and the riches of His love in Christ Jesus. It does not stand not on "its" and "ands," but on faith. It must undoubtedly, it must certainly be mine. And good reason, for this hope has a word to hang and hold on. What is that? I will wait on the Lord, and I hope in His Word, it is a Scripture hope, a Word hope. The word says, "The Lord came to save those that were lost." Why, I find myself to be lost, the soul says, and therefore I hope. The Lord will seek me, though I cannot seek him. I hope the Lord will find me, though I cannot find myself. I hope the Lord will save me, though I cannot save myself. So the Word says, "He appointed them that mourn in Zion, to give them beauty for ashes," (Isa. 61:3). Will you have a legacy of joy, mercy and pity? Here it is, the Lord Christ left it to you, I bequeath and leave this to all broken hearted sinners, to all you humble mourning sinners, this is your legacy, sue for it in court, and you shall have it forever.

2. A grounded hope is ever of great power and strength to hold the soul to the truth of the promise, hence take a poor sinner when he is at the weakest, under water, when all temptations, oppositions, corruptions grow strong against him, and he says, I shall one day perish by the hand of Saul, this proud, foolish heart of mine will be my bane, I shall never get power, strength and grace against these sins. Here is the

lowest under a poor soul. If a man should now reply, Then cast off all hope and confidence, reject the means, and turn to your sins. Mark how hope steps in, and says, No, whatsoever I am and do, whatsoever my condition is, I will use the means, I am sure all my help is in Christ, all my hope is in the Lord Jesus, and if I must perish, I will perish seeking Him, and waiting upon Him. Why, this is hope, and I warrant, that soul shall never go to hell. "I will wait for the Lord, yes though He hath hid Himself from the house of Jacob."

The last use is of exhortation. I desire you, I entreat you (I will not say, I command you, though this may be enjoined), if you have any hope of heaven, if you have any treasure in Christ, labor to quicken this affection above all. The means are these:

1. Labor to be much acquainted with the precious promises of God, to have them at hand, and on all occasions. These are you comforts, and will support your soul, as the body without comfort is unfit for anything. So it is here, unless a man has that provision of God's promises, and has them at hand daily, and has them dished out, and fitted for him, his heart will fail.

2. Maintain in your heart a deep and serious acknowledgment of that supreme authority of the Lord, to do what He wills, and how He wills, according to His pleasure. Alas, we think too often to bring God to our bow, we have

hoped this long, and God has not answered, and shall we wait still? Wait! Ah wait, and bless God that you may wait. If you may lie at God's feet, and put your mouths in the dust, and at the end of your days have one crumb of mercy, it is enough, therefore check those distempers, Shall I wait still? It is a most admirable strange thing, that a poor worm worthy of hell, should take up state, and stand upon terms with God. He will not wait upon God. Who must wait then? Must God wait, or man wait? It was the Apostle's question, "Wilt thou now restore the Kingdom of Israel?" to whom our Savior answered, "It is not for you to know the times and seasons," as who should say, hands off, it is for you to wait, and to expect mercy, it is not for you to know. If you begin to wrangle, and say, how long, Lord? When, Lord? And why not now, Lord? Why not I, Lord? Now check your own heart, and say, It is not for me to know, it is for me to be humble, abased, and to wait for mercy.

Section 4: We will now consider a desire and interest for Christ.

When the soul is humbled, and the eye opened, then he begins to reason in this way, O happy I that see mercy, but miserable I, if I come to see this, and never have a share in it! O, why not I (Lord?), why are not my sins pardoned? And why not my corruptions subdued? My soul now thirsts after thee as a thirsty land, my affections now hunger after righteousness both infused and imputed. Now this desire is begotten like this:

When the soul is come so far, that after a thorough conviction of sin, and found humiliation under God's mighty hand, it has a timely and seasonable revelation of the glorious mysteries of Christ, or His excellencies, invitations, truth, tenderheartedness, *etc.* of the heavenly splendor, and riches, of the pearl of great price. Then does the soul conceive by the help of the Holy Spirit, this desire and vehement longing. And (lest anyone deceive themselves by any misconception, as the notorious sinner, the mere civil man, and the formal professor), it is then known to be *saving*:

1. When it is joined with a hearty willingness and unfeigned resolution to sell all, to part with all sin, to bid adieu forever to our darling delight, it is not an effect of self-love, not an ordinary wish of natural appetite (like Balaam's, Numbers 23:10), of those who desire to be happy, but are unwilling to be holy, who would gladly be saved, but are loathe to be sanctified, no, if you desire earnestly, you will work accordingly, for as the desire is, so will the endeavor be.

2. When it is earnest, eager, vehement, extremely thirsting after Christ, as the parched earth for refreshing showers, or the hunted deer for water brooks. We read of a Scottish penitent, who a little before his confession, freely confessed his faults to the shame (as he said), of himself, and

to the shame of the devil, but to the glory of God, he acknowledged it to be so heinous, and horrible, that had he a thousand lives, and could die ten thousand deaths, he could not make satisfaction. Notwithstanding (he said), Lord, you have left me this comfort in the world, that you have said, come to me all ye that are weary and heavy laden, and I will refresh you. Lord, I am weary, Lord, I am heavy laden with my sins, which are innumerable, I am ready to sink, Lord, even into hell, unless you in your mercy put your hand to deliver me. Lord, you have promised by your own Word out of your own mouth, that you will refresh the weary soul. And with that he thrust out one of his hands, and reaching as high as he could towards heaven, with a louder voice and a strained voice, he cried, I challenge you, Lord, by that Word, and by that promise which you have made, that you perform and make it good to me, that call for ease and mercy at your hands, *etc.* Proportionately, when heavy heartedness for sin has so dried up the bones, and the angry countenance of God so parched the heart, that the poor soul begins now to gasp for grace, as the thirsty land for drops of rain, then the poor sinner (though dust and ashes), with a holy humility speaks to Christ, O merciful Lord God, You are *Alpha and Omega*, the beginning and the end, you say it is done, of things that are yet to come, so faithful and true are your decrees and promises. That you have promised by your own words out of your own mouth, that to him that is thirsty, you will give him of the fountain of the water of life freely. O Lord, I thirst, I faint, I languish, I long for one drop of mercy. *As the deer panteth for the waterbrooks, so panteth my soul after thee*, O God, and after the yearning bowels of they lacked compassions. Had I now in possession, the glory, the wealth, and pleasures of the whole world, no, had I ten thousand lives, joyfully would I lay them all down and part with them, to have this poor trembling soul of mine received into the bleeding arms of my blessed redeemer. O Lord, my spirit within me is melted into tears of blood, my heart is shivered into pieces, out of the very place of dragons, and shadow of death, do I lift up my thoughts heavy and sad before you, the remembrance of my former vanities and pollutions is a very vomit to my soul, and it is sorely wounded with the grievous representation thereof. The very flames of hell, Lord, the fury of your just wrath, the scorching of my own conscience, have so wasted and parched my heart, that my thirst is insatiable, my bowels are hot within me, my desire after Jesus Christ's pardon and grace, is greedy as the grave, the coals thereof are coals of fire, which has a most vehement flame. And, Lord, in your blessed *book* you call and cry, *Lo, every one that thirsteth, come ye to the waters*. In that great day of the feast, you stood and cried with your own mouth, if any man thirsts, let him come unto me and drink. And these are your own words, Those who hunger and thirst after righteousness shall be filled. I challenge thee, Lord, in this my most extreme thirst after your own blessed self, and spiritual life in you, by that Word, and by that promise which you have made, that you perform, and make it good to me, that lie groveling in the dust, and trembling at your feet. O! Open now that promised well of life, for I must drink, or else die.

The means to obtain this desire are *three:*

1. Be acquainted thoroughly with your own necessities and that which you lack, with that nothingness and emptiness that is in yourself, a groundless presumption makes a man careless. See into your own necessities; confess the lack of this desire after the Lord Jesus Christ.

2. Labor to spread forth the excellency of all the beauty and surpassing glory, that is in the promises of God. Could you but view them in their true light, they would ravish you, and quicken your desires.

3. After all this, know it is not in your power to bring your heart to desire Christ, you cannot hammer out a desire upon your own anvil, dig your own pit, and hew your own rock as long as you will. No, let all the angels in heaven, and all the ministers on earth provoke you, yet if the hand of the Lord is wanting, you shall not lift up your heart, nor step one step toward heaven, then go to Him who is able to work this desire in your soul. It is the complaint of a Christian, O they

are troubled, because they cannot fetch a good desire from their own souls, and one sinks, a third shakes, and they are overwhelmed with discouragement. What a wretched heart have I? Grace for me? No, no, the world I can desire, the life of my child I long for, and I say with Rachel, *Let me have honor or else I die.* But I cannot long for the inconceivable riches of the Lord Jesus Christ. And will the Lord show any mercy on me? Is it this way? Remember now, desires do not grow in your garden, they do not spring from the root of your abilities. O, seek God, and confess, in truth Lord, it is you from whom come all our desires, it is you who must work them in us as you have promised them to us. And therefore, Lord quicken this soul and enlarge this heart of mine, for you alone are the God of this desire. In this way, call down a desire from the Lord, and from the promise, for from there only it must come. The smoking flax God will not quench. Flax will not smoke, but a spark must come into it, and that will make it catch fire and smoke. In this way, lay your hearts before the Lord and say, Good Lord, here is only flax, here is only a stubborn heart, but strike it by your promise, from heaven that I may have a smoking desire after Christ, and after grace.

Section 5: Now we are to consider a Love of Christ.

We have run through two affections- hope and desire, and the next is love. A possible good stirs up hope, a necessary excellency sets up desire, and relishes in that good and kindles love. This is the order of God's work. If the good is absent, the understanding says, It is to be desired, O that I had it! Then it sends out hope, and it waits for that good, and stays till it can see it, and yet if that good cannot come, then desire has another proper work, and it goes up and down wandering, and seeks after Christ Jesus. After this, if the Lord Jesus is pleased to come Himself into the view of the heart, which longs this way after Him, saying, Lo, here is Jesus Christ the Messiah, that has ordered these great things for His saints and people. The motive or ground of this love is God's Spirit in the promise, letting in some intimation of God's love into the soul; Psalms 42:8, "The Lord will command His loving kindness in the day time." This is a phrase taken from kings and princes, and great commanders in the field, whose words of command stand for laws. So the Lord sends out His loving kindness, and faith. Go out, my everlasting love and kindness, take a commission from me, and go to that humble, thirsty and hunger-bitten sinner, and go and prosper, and prevail, and settle my love effectually upon him, and fasten my mercy on him. I command my loving kindness to do it. So the Lord does put a commission into the hands of His loving kindness, that it shall do good to the poor soul, even though it withdraws itself, saying, What, mercy for me? Will Christ Jesus accept me? No, no; there is no hope of mercy for me. Indeed, if I could pray this way, and hear and do everything I was supposed to, then there would be some comfort, but now there is no hope of mercy for me. We demand, is this your case? Are you humbled? Have you longed in this way for the riches of His mercy in Christ? Then, the Lord has put a commission into the hands of His loving kindness, saying, Go to that poor soul, and break open the doors upon that weary, weltering heart, and break off all the chains that hold it, and tear off the veil of ignorance and carnal reason, and all those arguments. Go, I say, to that soul, and cheer it, and warm it, and tell it from me. That his sins are pardoned, and his soul shall be saved, and his sighs and prayers are heard in heaven, and I charge you to do the work before you come again.

Here is the ground of love, God's love affecting the heart and settled on it. It breeds love back to God again. *We love Him because He loved us first.* The burning glass must receive heat of the beams of the sun, before it burns anything. So there must be a beam of God's love to fall on the soul, before it can love God again. I drew them with the cords of a man, even with the bands of love. God lets in the cords of love into the soul, and that draws love again to God. "He brought me into the banqueting house, his banner over me is love. Stay me with flagons; comfort me with apples, for I am sick with love," (Song of Songs 2:4-5). When the banner of Christ's love is spread over, the soul comes to be sick in love with Christ. Now this love of God begets our love in *three ways:*

First, there is a sweetness and relish which God lets into the soul, and warms the heart with. You shall see how the fire is kindled by and by. As when a man is fainting, we give him smelling salts to revive him, so a fainting sinner is cold at heart, and therefore the Lord lets in a drop of His loving kindness, and this warms the heart, and the soul is even filled with the happiness of the mercy of God. Let him kiss me with the kisses of his mouth (the spouse says in the Song of Songs), for his love is better than wine. The kisses of his mouth are comforts of His Word, and Spirit. The soul says, O let the Lord refresh me with the kisses of His mouth, let the Lord speak comfort to my heart, and this is better than wine.

Secondly, as that sweetness warms the heart, so the freeness of the love of God let in and intimated begins even to kindle this love in the soul, that it sparkles again. God sets out His love toward us, seeing that while we were yet sinners, Christ died for us. This commends the love of God, the Lord sends to poor and miserable, sinful broken-hearted sinners, and says, commend my mercy to such a one, and tell him, that though he has been an enemy to me, yet I am a friend to him, and though he has been rebellious against me, yet I am a God and Father to him. When the poor sinner considers this with himself, he says, is the Lord so merciful to me? I that loved my sins, and continued in them, had it not been just that I should have perished in them? But will the Lord not only spare His enemy, but give His Son for him? O, let my soul forever rejoice in this inconceivable goodness of God! Even though your heart be ever so hard, if it had but a sense of this, it cannot but stir you to humiliation.

Thirdly, the greatness of the freeness of this mercy of God, being settled on the heart, inflames it, the sweetness warms the heart, this freeness kindles the fire, and when the greatness of the sweetness comes to be valued, this sets the heart all on a flame, the Apostle desires, that the Ephesians being rooted and grounded in love, that they might be able to comprehend with all the saints, *what is the breadth and height of the love of God in Christ*, as if He had said, the immeasurableness of God's mercy will blow up the soul and enflame the heart with admirable love of God again, and will make the soul say, What, I that have done all that I could against this good God? O, it breaks my heart to think of it! There was no Name under heaven that I did not blaspheme and tear in pieces, more than this Name. No command under heaven I so much despised, as the command of God and of Christ, no Spirit that I grieved, so much as the good Spirit of God's and therefore had the Lord only given me a look, or spoken a word to me, it had been an infinite mercy, but to send his Son to save me. It is incomparable. I could not conceive to do so much evil against him, as he has done good to me. O, the breadth of that mercy beyond all limits! O, the length of that mercy beyond all time!

O, the depth of that mercy below a man's misery! O the height of that mercy above the height of my understanding! If my hands were all love, that I could work nothing but love, and if my eyes were able to see nothing but love, and my mind to think of nothing but love, and if I had a thousand bodies, they were all too little to love that God that has so immeasurably loved me a poor sinful hell-bound one. I will love the Lord dearly (David says), O Lord my strength. Have I gotten the Lord Jesus to be my comfort, my buckler and my shield? If I have any good, He begins it, if I have any comfort, He blesses it. Therefore, I will love you dearly, O Lord my strength, O how should I but love you!

I think there is a poor sincere soul that says, my understanding is not as deep as others, my tongue is not as glib, I am not able to so freely speak of the things of grace and salvation. I struggle, and cannot consistently engage in holy duties and services. I cannot dispute for a Savior or perform the spiritual duties that others can. Yet, sweet soul, can you love Christ Jesus, and rejoice in Him? O, yes! I bless the Name of the Lord, with all I have, all my friends, my parts, my means, my abilities, are like dung and dross in comparison to Christ Jesus. It is the comfort of my soul that I might ever be with him. Do you say this? Go your way, and the God of heaven go with you. This is a work that will never leave you, it is a badge and proper livery that the Lord Jesus gives only to his saints.

Never a mere professor under heaven ever wore it, nor a hypocrite, but only to those whom He has effectually called, and whom He will save. Therefore, though you lack the things of God, yet you do not have the ability to get them, you may say, I can say little for Christ, my tongue falters, and my memory is weak, yet the Lord knows I love the Lord Jesus. This is enough, David desired no more, but what God has purposed to do for His children that loved His Name, "Do to me (the text says), as you used to do to those that love your name; I know you love them that love you, and will save and glorify them in the end. I desire no more but this, do as you used to do to those that love your name." And does David, a king, desire no more than that? Sure then if you (poor soul), have as much as he had, it is enough, and be quiet with your child's part, your lot is fallen into a marvelous fair ground.

Some may say, this is all the difficulty, how may I know whether my love is a true love, or a false love? How may I know, that my love is of the right kind?

Let every man put his love on trial, and examine it this way, whether you welcome Christ and grace, according to their worth? If you do, it will appear in *this way:*

1. Observe the root and rise from which your love came, can you say, I love the Lord because He has first loved me? Then your love is of the right substance, and be assured it is forever, that God who cannot but love Himself, He cannot

but like the love that came from Himself. Is your soul affected and enlarged in love for the Lord, because you have felt and retained the relish and sweetness of His grace? Can you say, the Lord has let in a glimpse of His favor? And the Lord has said in His truth, He looks to Him that trembles at His word, the Minister said it, and the Spirit says it, that my mercy is registered in heaven. O, how should I love the Lord! My sins are many, which I have bewailed, my sighs and sobs I have put up to heaven, and at the last the Lord has given me a gracious answer. O how should I love the Lord my strength dearly? If it is this way with you, your love is sound, and will never fail.

2. If you entertain your Savior, as it befits him, you must entertain him as a king, and that is like this: give all to him, and entertain none other with him on terms of honor, but such as have him, and who attend on him, love everything about Christ, and for Christ, express your love and joy to Christ above all. He is as a King, and all the rest are empty, he that loves anything equal with Christ, it is certain he never did love Christ, to set up anything cheek by jowl with Christ, it is the same as if a man put a slave into the same chamber with the king, which is going to drive to the effect of driving him away.

The soul that rightly entertains Christ, and studies wholly to give Him contentment, he is marvelously wary and watchful, that he may not cause the Spirit of God to grieve him, and cause Him to go away displeased. See Song of Songs 3:4-5. The spouse fought long for her beloved, and at last brought him home, and when she had welcomed him, she give a charge to all the house, not to stir or awaken her love, until he wishes. When a prince comes to the house of a great man, there is a charge given to make no noise in the night, lest such and such a man be awakened before his time? The soul, when it has received the Spirit of the Lord Jesus Christ, does this, He gives a preemptory charge to keep watch and gives a charge to hope, desire, love and joy, and the mind, and all, not to grieve and molest the good Spirit of God, let there no motion but to entertain it, no advice but to receive it, and do nothing that may work the least kind of dislike to it.

4. He that truly entertains Christ, rejoices in the good and glory of Christ. When Mephibosheth had been wrongfully accused by David, and when David who had taken away all the inheritance from him, was returned to safety, then David said to comfort him, "Thou and Ziba divide the land. No, said Mephibosheth, Let him take all, for as much as my Lord the king is come again in peace, it matters not for inheritance, and for myself and my life, I pass not, since the King has returned in peace, it is enough that I enjoy thy preference, which is better to me than goods, life or liberty." So it is with a kind loving heart, which cannot endure to see Christ's honor and glory laid in the dust, but if His praise is

advance, then is he glad, Lord, I have enough (the soul says), that Christ is mine, and that His honor and glory is magnified, whatsoever becomes of me it does not matter, let the world take all, if I may have Christ, and see him praised and magnified. Let this try any man's spirit under heaven, and labor to bring the soul to this way of thinking. A minister in his place, and master in his place, and every Christian in his place, let it be our care to honor God, not ourselves, and let it be our comfort, if God may be better honored by others, than by ourselves. This is our business of Spirit, we can be content to lift up Christ on our shoulders, that we may lift up ourselves by it, but we should be content to lie in the dust, that the Lord may be praised, and if any of God's people thrive and prosper more than you, let that be your joy.

5. He that welcomes Christ truly, covets a nearer union with Christ. Love is a linking and gluing nature, and will carry the soul with some kind of strength and earnestness, to enjoy full possession and fellowship of the thing that is loved. It cannot have enough of it. Nothing (the soul says), but Christ, still I desire more of that mercy, and holiness, and grace, and love in Christ Jesus. As it is with parties that have lived long together in one house, and their affections are linked together, and to be drawing on the marriage, so the soul that loves Christ Jesus, and has his holy affection kindled, and his spirit enlarged in it, when the Lord

has let in some glimpse of His love, he thinks the hour is sweet when he prayed to the Lord Christ. He thinks the Lord's day sweet, in which God revealed, by the power of his holy ordinances, any of his rich grace and mercy. It is admirable to see how the heart will be delighted to recover the time and place, and means, when and where the Lord did reveal it, O this is good (the soul says), O that I might ever be in this way cheered and refreshed! Or as the spouse contracted, thinks every day a year, until she enjoy her beloved, and took satisfaction to her soul in him. So the soul that has been truly humbled and enlightened, and is now contracted to Christ Jesus, O when will that day be (it says), that I shall ever be with my Jesus! He takes hold of every word he hears, every promise that reveals anything of Christ, But oh! When will that day be, that I shall ever be with Christ, and be full of his fullness forever?

And now let me prevail with your hearts, and work your souls to this duty, Love the Lord, all ye his saints, whom will you love, if you do not love Him? O you poor ones, love the Lord, for you have cause, and you little ones too (if there is any such in the congregation), He knocks at every man's heart, and persuades every man's soul, *Love the Lord*.

The means are *these:*

1. Labor to give attendance daily to the promise of grace, and Christ; drive away all other suitors from the soul,

and let nothing come between the promise and it. Forbid all things that interfere, and let the promise confer daily with your heart, and be expressing and telling of that good that is in Christ, to your own soul. If all things are agreed between parties to be married, and there lacks nothing but mutual affection. The only way to fix their affections on one another is to keep company together, so as they meet wisely and holily. So let the soul daily keep company with the promise, and this is the first way.

2. Labor to be thoroughly acquainted with the beauty and sweetness of Christ in the promise. Now there are three things in the promise that we must eye and comprehend, so our hearts are kindled with love in the *Lord:*

1. The worth of the party in himself.

2. The deservingness of the party, that Christ deserves it.

3. The readiness of the party in Himself to seek our good, Christ seeks it.

1. Christ is worthy in Himself. If we had a thousand hearts to bestow on Him, we were never able to love Him sufficiently, as Nehemiah said, "The name of the Lord is above all praise;" will you let out your love and affections? You may lay them out here with good advantage. What would you love? Would you love beauty? Then your Savior is beautiful, "You are fairer than the children of men," Psalms 45:2. Would

you have strength? Then is your Savior strong, "Gird thy sword on thy thigh, O most mighty," Psalms 45:3. Would you have riches? Your Savior is rich (if it were possible), then He is strong, "He is heir of all things," Heb. 1:2. Would you have wisdom? Then your Savior is wise, yes wisdom itself, "In Him are hid the treasures of wisdom and knowledge." Col. 2:3. Would you have eternal life? Christ is the author of life and happiness to all that have Him, and He has not only these in Himself, but he will infuse you with them if you will but walk with Him.

2. Christ deserves our love, in regard to benefits toward us, be man never so worthy in Himself, yet if he has wronged, or expressed the part of an enemy, a woman says, I will not have him though he had all the world, this takes off the affections. It is not so with the Lord Jesus. As he is worthy of all love in himself, so he has dealt mercifully and graciously with you. In your sickness, who helped you? In wants, who supplied you? In anguish of heart, who relieved you? It was Jesus Christ. O therefore love him, deal equally with him, as He deserves, so enlarge your hearts to him forever.

3. Christ seeks our love. Here is the admiration of mercy, that our Savior, who has been rejected by a company of sinful creatures, should seek their love. For shame do not refuse him, but let him have love as he would. Had the lord received us, when we had come to him, and humbled our

hearts before him, had he heard, when we had spent our days, all our strength in begging and craving, it had been an infinite mercy. But when the Lord Jesus Christ shall seek us by His messengers (it is all the work we have to do to woo you and speak a good word for the Lord Jesus Christ, yes, and if we speak for ourselves, it is pity but our tongue should cleave to the roof of our mouth), when the Lord Jesus shall come and wait on us, and seek our love, O this is the wonder of mercies! Think of this, O you saints! The Lord now, by us offers love to all you that are weary and have need. What answer shall I return to him in the evening? Shall I say, Lord, I have tendered your mercy, and it was refused? Brethren, it would grieve my heart to return this answer. O rather, let every soul of yours say, can the Lord Jesus love me? In truth, Lord, I am in love with myself, I have abused your majesty, I have loved the world, I have followed base lusts, and can the Lord Jesus love such a wretch as I am? Yet says the Lord, I will heal their backsliding, I will love them freely. He looks for not portion, he will take you and all your wants. Get home then, and every one in secret, labor to deal truly with your own hearts. Match them up like this, and say, Is it possible that the Lord should look so low? That a great prince should send to a poor peasant, that majesty should stoop so low? Heaven to earth, God to man? Has the Lord offered mercy to me? And does he require nothing of me but to love him again? Call on your hearts, I charge you, and say this, Lord, again? Call on your hearts, I charge you, and say this, Lord, if all the light of my eyes were love, and all the speeches of my tongue were love, it was all too little to love you. O let me love you dearly! If you will not say this, then say hereafter, you had a fair offer, and that a poor minister of God did well trying to express it. Alas, be not coy and squeamish, the Lord may have better than you, lie down therefore, and admire at the mercy of the Lord, that he should take a company of dead dogs, and now at the last, say as the Prophet did, "Lift up your heads, O ye gates! And be ye lifted up, ye everlasting doors, and the King of Glory shall come in."

Section 6: Next we will consider relying on Christ.

We have now come to the work of the will, which is the great wheel and commander of the soul. The former affections were but as handmaids to usher in Christ and the promises. The mind says, I have seen Christ. Hope, faith, I have waited. Desire says, I have longed. Love says, I am kindled. Then says the will, I will have Christ, it shall be so. And this makes up the match, the spawn and seeds of faith that went before, now faith is come to some perfection, now the soul reposes itself on the Lord Jesus.

And this reposing or resting itself, discovers a fivefold *act:*

First, it implies a going out of the soul to Christ. When the soul sees this, that the Lord Jesus is his aid, and must ease him and pardon his sins, then let us go to that Christ, he says, it is the Lord's call, "Come to me all ye that are weary." Now this voice coming home to the heart, and the prevailing sweetness of the call over-powering the heart, the soul goes out, and falls, and flings itself on the riches of God's grace.

Secondly, it lays hold fast on Christ. When the Lord says, "Come my love, my dove, O come away! Behold, I come" (she says), and when she is come, she fastens on Christ, saying, "My beloved is mine, and I am his." Faith lays hold on the Lord, and will not let mercy go, but cleaves to it, though it conflicts with the Lord, "Should he slay me (Job says), yet will I trust in Him." The case is like Benhadads, who being overcome by Ahab, his servants thus advise him, "We have heart that the kings of Israel are merciful kings, we pray thee let us put ropes about our necks, and sackcloth on our loins, and go out to the king, peradventure he will save your life." So the servants go, and coming to Ahab, they deliver the message, "Thy servant Benhadad saith, I pray thee let me live." And he said, "Is he yet alive? He is my brother. Now the men diligently observed whether any thing would come from him, and did hastily catch at it, and they said, your brother Benhaddad, and they went away rejoicing." This is the lively picture of a broken hearted sinner, after he has taken up arms against the Almighty, and that the Lord has let in justice, and he sees (or has seen), the anger of God bent against him. Then the soul reasons, I have heard, though I am a rebellious sinner, that none but sinners are pardoned, and God is a gracious God, and therefore unto him let me go. With this he falls down at the footstool of the Lord, and cries, O what shall I do! What shall I say unto you? O you preserver of men! O let me live, I pray you, in the sight of my Lord! The soul in this way is humbled, then the Lord lets in His sweet voice of mercy, and says, you are my son, my love, and your sins are pardoned. These words no sooner uttered, but he catches himself saying, Mercy, Lord? And a son, Lord? And love, Lord? And a pardon, Lord? The heart holds itself here, and will never fall away.

Thirdly, it casts the weight of all its occasions and troubles, guilt and corruptions, on the Lord Jesus Christ. He that walks in darkness does not have light, let him trust in the name of the Lord, and stay on His God. That is, if a man is in extremity, hopeless in misery, and walks in desperate discouragements, and has no comfort, let him trust in the name of the Lord, and stay on his God. As when a man cannot go by himself, he lays all the weight of his body on another, so the soul goes to Christ, and lays all the weight of itself on Christ, and says, I have no comfort, O Lord, all my discomforts and consolation. Who is this, says Solomon, that comes up from the wilderness, leaning on her beloved, Song of Songs

8:5. The party coming is the church, the wilderness is the troubles and vexations the church meets throughout, and the beloved is the Lord Jesus Christ. Now the church leans herself on her husband, she walked along with Him, but he bore all the burden. "Cast all your care on Him, (Peter says), for He careth for you." 1 Pet. 5:7. The original is, "hurl your care on the Lord." The Lord will not thank you for carrying your cares and troubles about you, he requires that you hurl them on him, for he cares for you.

Fourthly, it draws virtue, and derives power from the Lord Jesus Christ for succor and supplies, and here is the special life of faith, it seeks for mercy, and grace, and comfort in Christ, he knows 'tis to be had from him, and therefore he fetches all from him, "With joy shall ye draw water out of the wells of salvation," Isa. 12:3. The fountain of salvation is Christ, and all the waters of life, of grace and mercy, are in Christ Jesus. Now, it is not enough to let down the bucket into the well, but it must be drawn out also. It is not enough to come to Christ, but we must draw the water of grace from Christ to ourselves, "They shall suck and be satisfied (Isaiah says), with the breaths of her consolations, that they may milk out, and be delighted with the abundance of her glory." The church is compared to a child, and the breasts are the promises of the gospel. Now the elect must suck, and be satisfied with them. The word in the original is, "Exact on the promise, and oppress the promise." As the oppressor grinds the face of a poor man, so with a holy kind of oppression, you should exact from the promise, and get what good you may from it.

Fifthly, faith leaves the soul with promise. Yet, notwithstanding all delays, denials, discouragements from God, faith brings on the heart still, it will be sure to lie at the gate, and keep the soul with the promise, whatever befalls it. Excellent is that passage, Gen. 32:26 when the Lord and Jacob were wrestling, "Let me go saith the Lord, I will leave thee to your self, I care not what becomes of thee." No, "I will not let thee go, until you have blessed me," says Jacob. So the faithful soul lays hold on the Lord for mercy and pardon and subdues graciously these cursed corruptions, which I am not able to master myself." As it is with a sundial, the needle is ever moving, and a man may jog it this way and that way, yet it will never stand still, till it comes to the north point. So, when the Lord leaves off a believing heart with frowns, and with the expression of displeasure, and the soul turns to the Lord Christ, and will never leave till it goes God-ward, and Christ-ward, and grace-ward, and faith-ward, Let the Lord do what he pleases, I will go no further, until he is pleased to show mercy. So once the soul comes to Christ, it will never go away, but ever cleaves to the promise, and is towards God and Christ, whatever befalls it.

But (poor soul), are you yet shut up in unbelief? Do then as the prisoner in Newgate, what lamentable cries do they utter to every passenger going by? So do you, look out from the gates of hell, and from under the bars of infidelity, and cry, that God would look on you with mercy, and say, spare, Lord, a poor unbelieving wretch, locked up under the bars of unbelief, good Lord succor, and deliver in your good time. David could say, let the sighting of prisoners come up before you. That indeed was meant of bodily imprisonment, yet the argument prevails much in regard of the spiritual. Good Lord, let the sighing of prisoners come up before you. Let the sighing of poor distrustful souls come up before your majesty. O send help from heaven, and deliver the soul of your servant from these wretched distempers of heart. Is there no cause to pray? He that does not believe (the Savior says), is condemned already. He is cast in heaven and earth, by the law and gospel, there is no relief for him abiding in this condition. Lay this under your pillow, and say, how can I sleep and be a condemned man? What if God should take away my life this night? Alas! I never knew what it was to be enlightened or wounded for sin. I can commit sin, and play with sin, but I never knew what it was to be wounded for sin. I never knew what it was to be zealous in a good cause. O, I confess I have no faith at all! Beloved! Would you yield this, then were there some hope that you might get out of this condition and state, to have a sense of its lack, to go to the Lord by prayer, and to ask heartily counsel of some faithful minister, which are the first steps to obtain it. And to help a poor wretch in this case, O you that are gracious, go your way home, and pray for him. Brethren, let us leave preaching and hearing, and all of us fall to praying and mourning. In truth, I condemn my own soul, because I have not a heart to mourn for him. We reprove his sin, and condemn him for his sin, and we do so, but where are the heart blood petitions that we put up for such a one? Where are the tears that we make for the slain of our people? You tender-hearted mothers, and you tender-hearted wives, if your children or husbands are in this woeful situation, O, mourn for them, let your hearts break over them, and say, O, woe is me for my children, O woe is me for that poor husband of mine!

Or secondly, have you gotten faith? Then labor to husband this grace well, and to improve it for your best good. It is a marvelous shame, to see those that are born to humble circumstances (I mean the poor saints of God), that have a right and title to grace and Christ, and yet to live in such an underrated way. I would have you to live above the world, for the Lord does not grudge his people of comfort, but would have them live cheerfully, and have strong consolations, and a mighty assurance of God's love. Is this not cause? Why, faith, if it is right, will make the life of the Christian most easy, most comfortable. Unfaithful souls sink in their sorrows on every occasion, but faith gives ease to a man in all his conversation. 1. Because faith has a skill, and a kind of flight, to put over all cares to another. We take up the cross, but faith hurls all the care on Christ, it is an easy matter to live under the burden, when another bears all the weight of it. Look how it is with two ferrymen, the one hales his boat about the shore, and cannot get off, but tugs and pulls, and never puts her forth to the tide. The other puts his boat on the stream, and sets up his sail, and then he may sit still in his boat, and the wind will carry him wherever he is to go. Just as it is with a faithful soul, and with an unbeliever. All the care of the faithful soul, is put into the stream of God's providence, and so he goes on cheerfully, because it is not he that carries him, but the Lord Jesus Christ. Whereas, every unfaithful soul tugs and pulls at the business, and can find neither ease nor success. Alas! He thinks by his own wits or power he can do what he wills.

2. Because faith *sweetens* all other afflictions, even those that are most hard and full of tediousness, and however it apprehends all troubles and afflictions, yet with it apprehends the faithfulness of God, ordering all for our good. And that is the reason why all our troubles are digested comfortably, without any harshness at all. When the patient takes better pills, if they are well sugared they go down easier, and the bitterness never troubles him. So it is with faith, it takes away

the harshness of all inconveniences, which are bitter pills in themselves, but they are sweetened and sugared over by the faithfulness of God, for the good of the soul, and therefore it goes on cheerfully.

You will say, if faith brings such ease, how may a man that has faith improve it to have such comfort for it? I answer, the rules are *four:*

1. Labor to gain some evidence to your own soul, that you have a title to the promise. The reason why poor Christians go drooping, are overwhelmed with their sins and miseries is because they do not see their title to mercy, nor their evidence of God's love to the word and to the testimonies. Take on evidence from the Word, it is as good as a thousand, if you shall have but one promise for you, you have all in truth, though all are not so fully and clearly perceived.

2. Labor to set a high price on the promises of God. One promise, and the sweetness of God's mercy in Christ, is better than all the honors or riches in the world. Prize these at this rate, and you cannot choose but to find ease and be contented.

3. Labor to keep your promises ever at hand. What is it to me if I have a thing in the house, if I have it but cannot find it? If a man is ready to die, say, I have as good cordial water as any in the world, but I do not know where it is. He may die before he can find it. So when misery comes, and your heart is

burdened, O then some promise, some comfort comes to bear up a poor fainting, drooping soul, for my troubles are many and I cannot bear them. Why now Christ and a promise would have done it, but you have thrown them in the corner, and they are not to be found. Now for the Lord's sake let me entreat you to be wise, for your poor soul, there is many a fainting and anguishing fit that comes over the heart of many a poor Christian, persecutions from without, and sorrows and corruptions from within, therefore keep your faith about you, and be sure that you have it within reach. Take hold of it, and bring more and be refreshed by it, and go singing to your grave, and to heaven forever.

4. Labor to drink in a hearty draught of the promise, bestow yourself on the promise every hour, whenever you do find a fit of discouragement coming, and this is the way to find comfort. Eat O friends, and drink, ye abundantly, O beloved. The original is "in drinking drink." You cannot be drunk with the Spirit, as you may with wine, drink abundantly, as if dainties were prepared. If a hunger-starved man comes in, and takes only a bit away, he must go away hungry. Think of it sadly, you faithful saints of God, you may come now and then, and take a snatch of promise, and then comes fear, and temptation, and persecution, and all quiet is gone again, it is your own fault brethren, you come thirsty, and go away thirsty, you come discomforted, and so you go away. Many

times it so befalls us ministers, when we preach of consolation, and when we pray, and confer, we think we are beyond all trouble; but by and by we are full of fears, troubles, and sorrow, because we do not take full contentment in the promise, we do not drink a deep draught of it. Of this take heed, too. 1. Of caviling and quarrelling with carnal reason. 2. Of attending to the parlays of Satan's temptations; if we listen to this chat, he will make us forget all our comfort.

CHAPTER 7: THE GROWING OF THE SOUL WITH CHRIST

Therefore, we have spoken of the soul's implantation, especially of the putting to the soul into Christ. We have now come to the second, which is, the growing of the soul with Christ. These two take up the nature of engrafting a sinner into the stock of Christ Jesus. Now this growing together is accomplished by *two means:*

1. By a union of the soul with Christ.

2. By a conveyance of sap or sweetness (all the treasures of grace and happiness), that is in Christ to the soul.

First, every believer is joined to Christ, and so joined or knit, that he becomes one spirit. 1. He is joined, as a friend to a friend, as a father to a child, a husband to a wife, as a graft to a tree, as the soul to a body. So is Christ to a believer, "I live, not I, but the Lord Jesus liveth in me." Here, the body of the faithful is called "Christ," 1 Cor. 12:12. 2. So jointed that the believer comes to be one spirit with Christ. This mystery is great, and beyond the reach of that little light I enjoy. Only I shall communicate what I conceive, in these three following conclusions: 1. that the Spirit of God (third person of the

Trinity), does really accompany the whole Word, but more especially the precious promises of the gospel.

2. The Spirit (accompanying the promise of grace and salvation), it does it by supernatural strength and power, a spiritual and overpowering virtue on the soul, and by it carries, it, and brings forth Christ. It is not so much anything in the soul, as a spiritual assisting, and moving, and working on the soul, by virtue of it being moved and carried to the Lord Jesus Christ. 3. The Spirit of grace in the promise, working this way on the heart, it causes the heart to close the heart to close with the promise, and with itself in the promise, and this is to be one spirit. As it is with the moon (the philosopher observes, that the ebbing and flowing of the sea, is by virtue of the moon), she flings her beams into the sea, and not being able to exhale as the son does, she leaves them there, and goes away, and that draws them, and when they grow wet, they return back again. Now the sea ebbs and flows, not from any principle in itself, but by virtue of the moon. So the heart of a poor creature is like the water, unable to move towards heaven, but the Spirit of the Lord does bring in its beams, and leave a supernatural virtue by them on the soul, and by it draws it to itself.

Here, a use of instruction. This may show us that the sins of the faithful are grievous to the blessed Spirit, to be one Spirit with Christ. Should a wife not only entertain a whoremonger into the house but also lodge him in the same bed with her husband, this is not to be endured, and will you receive a company of base lusts, and that in the very face and sight of the Lord Jesus Christ? What? Lodge an unclean spirit, with the clean Spirit of the Lord! The Holy Spirit cannot endure this. "Let no filthy communication come out of your mouth," Eph. 4:29. What is there to do, you may say. What? A Christian and a liar? A Christian and a swearer? O do not grieve the Holy Spirit of God, because by it you are sealed to the day of redemption. The good Spirit of the Lord has sealed you unto redemption, and knit you into Himself, and will you rend yourselves from him and grieve him? *O grieve not* the Holy Spirit!

2. For examination, if your heart is estranged from such as walk consistently before God, because they are humble and faithful, it is an ill sign. When they are made one spirit with Christ, will you be of two spirits with them? I confess a godly heart will have his fits and excursions now and then, but this while this is poison, and the soul of a godly man sees this and is weary of it, and is marvelously burdened by it, and says, O vile wretch that I am, what would I have! And what is He, that I cannot love Him? Is it because the good Spirit of the Lord is there? Shall I resist the good Spirit of the Lord? And so commit the sin against the Holy Spirit? Away you vile, wretched heart, I will love him. So the soul labors

and strives for the exactness, and would regularly have that goodness which he sees in another.

Secondly, as there is a union with Christ, so there is a conveyance of all spiritual grace from Christ, to all those that believe in him. If you would know the tenure of this covenant, and how Christ conveys these spiritual graces to us, it discovers itself in these ways. 1. There is fully enough in the Lord Jesus Christ for every faithful soul. 2. As there is enough in Christ, so Christ does supply or communicate whatsoever is most fit. 3. As the Lord does communicate what is fit, so he does preserve what he does bestow and communicate. 4. As the Lord does preserve what he communicates, so he quickens the grace that He now does preserve. 5. As the Lord quickens what he preserves, so he never leaves until he perfects what he quickens. 6. As the Lord perfects what he quickens, so in the end he crowns all the grace he has perfected. And now may I read what you have been granted, you poor saints of God, you who live beggarly and basely here. O! If you have a Savior you are made forever, it is that which will maintain you, not only Christianly, but triumphantly, what you want, Christ has, and what is fit, Christ will bestow, if you cannot keep it, He will preserve it for you. If you are sluggish, He will quicken it in you. What would you have more? He will perfect what he quickens, and lastly, he will crown what he perfects, he will give you an immortal crown of glory forever and ever.

Here we see whether the saints of God should go to fetch, succor and supply of whatsoever grace they lack, yes, increase and perfection of what they have already. Christ is made all in all to His servants. Why then, away to the Lord Jesus, He calls and invites, I counsel you to buy of me eye salve if you have been an accursed man, buy of Christ's justification, if you are a polluted creature, buy of Christ's sanctification. With you is the wellspring of life (David says), and in your light we shall only see light. It is not with us, but with you, it is not in our heads, or hearts, or performances, it is only in Christ to be found, only from Christ to be fetched. I do not deny but we should improve all means, and use all helps, but in the use of all, seek only to Christ, with Him is the well of life, away to Christ, wisdom, righteousness, *etc.* all is in Him, and there we must have them.

You will say, what are the means to obtain these graces from Christ? I answer. First, eye the promise daily, and keep it within view. Secondly, yield yourself, and give way to the stroke of the promise, and to the power of the Spirit. For instance, imagine that your heart begins to be pestered with vain thoughts, or with a proud haughty spirit, or some base lusts and privy haunts of the heart, how would you be rid of these? You must not quarrel, and contend, and be discouraged. No, but eye the promise, and hold fast to it, and say, Lord, you have promised all grace to your servants, take this heart, and this mind, and these affections, and let your spirit frame them aright according to your own good will, by that Spirit of Wisdom (Lord), inform me, by that Spirit of sanctification (Lord), cleanse me from all my corruptions, by that Spirit of grace (Lord), quicken and enable me to the discharge of every holy service. So carry yourself, and convey your soul by the power of the Spirit of the lord, and you shall find your heart strengthened and succored by the virtue of it on all occasions.

For conclusion, to drive this use deeper into your hearts, if every believer is joined with Christ, and from Christ there be a conveyance of all spiritual grace to every believer, then above all labor for Christ in all things. Never let your heart is quieted, never let your soul be contented until you have obtained Christ. Take a malefactor on whom sentence is passed, and execution is to be administered, and suggest to him how to be rich, or how to be pardoned, how to be honored, he will tell you, riches are good, and honors are good, but oh, a pardon is all I want. Ah, but then should you say, he must leave all for a pardon. He will answer again, take all and give me a pardon, that I may live, though in poverty, that I may live, though in misery. So it is with a poor believing soul, every man that has committed sin, must suffer for sin, says justice, the sentence is passed, every man that does not believe is condemned already, says the Savior, what would you have now? You say, you would have a pardon, but would you not rather have riches? Alas! What is that to me (the soul says), to be rich and a *reprobate*? Honored and *damned*? Let me be pardoned, though impoverished, let me be justified, though debased, yet though I never see a good day. Why then labor for a Christ, for there is no other way under heaven, get a broken heart, get a believing heart, but O above all, get Christ to justify you, get Christ to save you. If I could pray like an angel, could I hear and remember all the sermons, could I confer as of no man had ever spoken, what is that to me, if I do not have Christ? I may go down to hell for all that have or do, yet take this along, and understand me aright, Christ is not only Savior of all His, but He is the God of all grace, as He is the God of all pardoning, so He is the God of all purging and purifying to the soul of each believer. Grace therefore is good, and duties are good, seek for all, we should do so, perform all, we ought to do so, but O, Christ, Christ, Christ in all, above all, more than all. Thus I have shown the way to the Lord Jesus, I have shown you also how you may come to be implanted into the Lord Jesus, and now I leave you in the hands of a Savior, in the bowels of a redeemer, and I think I cannot leave you better.

Soli Deo Gloria.

FINIS

www.ingramcontent.com/pod-product-compliance
Lightning Source LLC
Chambersburg PA
CBHW020400100426
42812CB00001B/141
* 9 7 8 0 2 6 8 0 2 1 6 8 9 *